Education for Holistic Transformation in Africa

Education for Holistic Transformation in Africa

FAUSTIN NTAMUSHOBORA

Foreword by Victor Babajide Cole

WIPF & STOCK · Eugene, Oregon

EDUCATION FOR HOLISTIC TRANSFORMATION IN AFRICA

Copyright © 2015 Faustin Ntamushobora. All rights reserved. Except for brief quotations in critical publications or reviews, no part of this book may be reproduced in any manner without prior written permission from the publisher. Write: Permissions. Wipf and Stock Publishers, 199 W. 8th Ave., Suite 3, Eugene, OR 97401.

Wipf and Stock
An Imprint of Wipf and Stock Publishers
199 W. 8th Ave., Suite 3
Eugene, OR 97401

www.wipfandstock.com

ISBN 13: 978-1-4982-0010-3

Manufactured in the U.S.A. 04/01/2015

Contents

Preface | vii
Foreword by Victor Babajide Cole | ix

1. The Need for Education for Holistic Transformation in Africa | 1
2. Brief History of Education in Africa | 10
3. Theory of Education for Holistic Transformation | 33
4. Biblical and Theological View of Holistic Transformation | 71
5. Holistic Transformation in Africa: Findings from Research in Kenya | 97

Appendix A: Description of Sampled Universities | 119
Appendix B: Research Questions | 122
Appendix C: Letter to and Responses from Universities Sampled | 124
Appendix D: Profile of Interview Participants | 130

Bibliography | 133
Index | 143

Preface

My interest in holistic transformation is tied to a long history in my life. In the 1980s I had an opportunity to coordinate fifty-two projects of Compassion International in Rwanda. Compassion International is a ministry that cares for the needs of a child in a holistic way. I was thrilled to see children and families transformed through a relationship of people from both sides of the ocean, and children growing in the love of God as their other needs were being met. By that time I did not understand much about transformation, but I could observe that Compassion International was different from other ministries that dichotomized the human being.

In 1986 I resigned from Compassion International and went to Shalom University in Bunia, Democratic Republic of Congo, to study theology. It was during my undergraduate studies that I was exposed to the dichotomizing of the evangelicals and to their Lausanne Confession, 1974. The Lausanne confession of 1974 text opened my eyes to education and discipleship in Africa and their failure, generally speaking, to impact change in community. It was also during my undergraduate training that I came across the expression "the church in Africa is a mile long and an inch deep," although this is not just for Africa. When I went back to Rwanda after my first degree, it was evident to me that the church in Rwanda was growing in numbers but less in quality. It was because of this reason that in 1992, Gary Scheer, a missionary friend from World Venture (CB International then) and I founded the New Creation Ministries whose vision was to mentor small teams of leaders with in-depth biblical training and equipping them to disciple others. Two years later, Gary and I were proven to be right; within a hundred days, almost a million Rwandans were killed by fellow Rwandans, and most of the killers claimed to be Christians. Were the killers really Christians? A true Christian is a disciple of Christ; does a disciple kill or love? The genocide raised in me more questions about the need of the church in Africa to impact society.

Preface

As a result of these questions, when I went to Daystar University I wrote my master's thesis on discipleship through relationships. I was wrestling with the issue of heart transformation and I was convinced that the church in Africa and especially in Rwanda was giving facts and information instead of making disciples of Jesus Christ. Discipleship is a relationship with self, God and others. I thought about how the African worldview centered on relationship offered opportunity for discipleship, but, unfortunately, this opportunity was not taken advantage of. I read again and again the call of Jesus for the disciples to be with him and to learn through a relationship with him and with one another, and I was puzzled that Jesus' way was not the way discipleship was conducted in Africa. If you ask a hundred Christians in Rwanda whether they have gone through discipleship, they would say yes. If you ask them to explain how, I am pretty sure that 95 percent would tell you that they memorized the catechumen before their baptism, and that baptism marked the end of their discipleship. Is that what discipleship is all about?

In addition to spiritual transformation, my master's degree program opened my eyes to the importance of integration and the failure for western education to acknowledge that Africans are holistic by nature, and that, for Africans, there is no separation of spiritual and social, but all is integrated to make life abundant. I even understood this better, when I took a course on Church and community development. That was the peak of my paradigm shift in my worldview about transformation. After my master's degree I began reading books and articles with holistic transformation lenses but God wanted to equip me even more. In 2002 I joined African Leadership and Reconciliation Ministry (ALARM, Inc.), and for five years I ministered to leaders in East Africa using the holistic transformation development framework. In 2007 I went to the States where I did my doctoral studies in education at Biola University. My goal was to understand further what holistic transformation is, and how disciples of Christ can think critically, love the Lord and one another, and at the same time be change agents in their communities. At the end of my program, I wrote a doctoral dissertation on education for holistic transformation in Africa which I have transformed into this book. I am still learning how to form disciples who can bring holistic transformation on this continent of great potential, and I hope that my contribution will help the reader, especially Christian educators, to gain more understanding on holistic transformation and the method leading to it.

Amahoro—Shalom!

Foreword

This book, a purely "exploratory" exercise, is a timely contribution to the ongoing search for relevance in the formal education sector in Africa. For that reason the author devotes necessary space to the interface between education in traditional, colonial and post-colonial Africa in chapter 2. In any society, education serves specified purposes, not least the socialization of the young into a society's ideals; that I term "the *particular*." The author presents salient characteristics of traditional African education that point to a deliberate effort to achieve holistic education. While traditional education served its purpose for a time, sometimes still longed for today, that era no longer exists! Change, inherent in the nature of education, is inevitable. However, disruption and disregard for wholesome traditional values in the wake of acculturation, adaptation and assimilation of Western forms of education are truly lamentable. In an increasingly globalized world, there is the need to balance the particular with the *general*, the local with the *universal*—a tension that the author briefly alludes to in chapter 1. When this tension goes unresolved, it sometimes makes some educationists in Africa to lament the state of schooling, or even the African psyche, as shown in what the author quotes as "psychological ambivalence" in chapter 2. The consequential negative turn of events in the educational systems well chronicled in chapter 1 may however not always be justifiably blamed on historical antecedents. Rather, the situation provides ongoing formidable challenge to African educationists, which challenge John Hanson (1965) long spoke of, at a time when the wave of independence was sweeping across Africa. Hanson had challenged African educationists to do a critical re-think of Western education by differentiating between what is "hallucination and imagination in African education."

A niche of this volume is an attempt to promote holistic education, not just as information, but for transformation. To that end the author in

Foreword

chapter 3 explores leading theories for holistic transformation—graduating from Mezirow—perspective transformation (purely cognitive) to engaging multiple dimensions of being, as in Taylor and Brookfield (cognitive, affective, spiritual, intuitive *and* communal). But the non-Christian social scientist tends to bifurcate religiosity and spirituality. All these necessitated the author, in his quest for holism, to add in chapter 4, in a brilliant fashion, a theological perspective on holistic education. In the process, he acknowledges points of continuity between social science theories and biblical-theological perspective on education, but he also underscores the points of discontinuity. The author well underscores the critical and catalytic role of the *relational*, and in particular that of the community-of-learning—whether a faith community or a mentor-mentee relationship. The author's introduction of a biblical distinctive in the transformation process, namely "authenticity," is refreshing. While being categorical that it is the Holy Spirit who works transformation in individual learners, the teacher's role in facilitating that work is nevertheless well articulated. I cannot agree more with the author.

Ntamushobora in chapter 5 reports findings of his field-work among selected Christians, who had completed post-graduate studies from public and private (Christian) universities in Kenya. He compares his field results with the characteristics of wholesome African traditional education outlined in chapter 1 and the salient points of social science theories on transformation discussed in chapter 3. The findings show that in the course of their graduate studies, these graduates had experienced transformation entirely in line with social science theories, with a singular point of departure, namely their acknowledgement of the role of the Holy Spirit in the transformation process. As they self-reflected on their days as students, they also resonated very well, in their experience, with most characteristics of traditional African education, except in one area—that their graduate studies failed to connect them with their cultural heritage. However, an equally explicit comparison of the field results with the cardinals of biblical-theological perspectives on transformation begs.

I highly commend this book to all who strive for greater relevance and holistic education as transformation, whether in Africa or beyond.

Victor Babajide Cole
Professor of Curriculum Development & Evaluation
Africa International University, Nairobi

1

The Need for Education for Holistic Transformation in Africa

INTRODUCTION

The position of the African continent in the world today marked by globalization requires that education in higher learning institutions, whether Christian or secular, be geared toward preparing graduates to face the challenges of the moment. Africa needs education that can face its multifaceted spiritual, social, economic and environmental problems. The African traditional education, though it was effective in propagating the cultural values of the African society, alone can no longer stand the challenges of globalization. Neither can the formal education introduced by colonizers, which was substandard compared to the European level,[1] and whose methods were based on transmission of information without critical thinking. Akilagpa states, "The principal contribution of a university to society turns on the quality of the knowledge it generates and imparts, the habits of critical thought and problem-solving it institutionalizes and inculcates in its graduates, and the values of openness and democratic governance it promotes and demonstrates."[2] My assertion is that African universities will make an impact on society only if to Akilagpa's three above

---

1. See Kelly, *French Colonial Education*; Mungazi, *Colonial Education for Africans*.
2. Akilagpa, "Challenges Facing African Universities," 26.

constructs—quality of knowledge, habit of critical thinking, and value of openness—can be added the use of African pedagogical methods which were transformative in nature and which fit the African worldview.

An example of such method is depicted in the following scenario of a mother, here named Mukamana, mentoring her two daughters: Iradukunda, the young one, and Hagenimana, the older one:

Mukamana: Have you finished cleaning all the dishes?

Iradukunda: Yes, we finished quite a while back. There were not many dishes today. We have not had as many visitors as we did in the last two days.

Hagenimana: Mother, why do these people like coming to our home? I do not see them going to other homes as much as they come to ours!

Mukamana: Do not ask such questions. Don't you know that visitors bring blessings and good fortune? Haven't you ever heard that *Urugo ni urugendwa* ("blessed is the home frequently visited")? When people come to visit us they also bring us news from the distant lands. You remember, for instance, when mother Kanyange was here, she told us that your aunt's daughter of the seventh ridge got married to a rich man and they have a baby boy now!

Iradukunda: Mother, Hagenimana does not like washing dishes and that is why she is complaining about visitors.

Mukamana: What kind of woman will you make, Hagenimana? Don't you know the proverb that says, *Urugo rwiza rwakira abashyitsi* ("a good home provides for the hungry")? A woman who is growing up almost ready to be married should not hate visitors nor refuse to offer them food. This is not good for a respectable wife.

Hagenimana: Mother, I have heard and I will not repeat it again.

Mukamana: Yes, if you hate visitors, your home will be like a deep river. But if you welcome visitors, good will shall always be with you. You will get people to tell you about distant lands and events coming up in the community. You will also get someone to scratch your back. My daughters, I would like you to be hardworking so that you will get good men to marry you. No one wants to marry a lazy girl. You go to bed now so that you will rise early to fetch water before going to the farm.[3]

This is an informal pedagogical method that the mother uses to inculcate knowledge, wisdom, values and tradition in her two daughters that

---

3. Ntamushobora, *From Trials to Triumphs*, 60.

The Need for Education for Holistic Transformation in Africa

she is preparing for life in the family and community at large. African traditional pedagogical methods were relevant and practical.

Illustrating the relevance of non-formal education in Africa, Gillespie and Melching conducted research in a non-government organization called Tostan (meaning "breakthrough" in Wolof) situated in Senegal.[4] The word Tostan in Wolof describes the sharing and spreading of knowledge by people themselves in their own language and using their own cultural traditions.[5] The curriculum of this organization was learner-centered and culture-based. The curriculum effectively integrated traditional West African proverbs, songs, stories, plays and dances into its pedagogical approach, and learners were involved in the development and implementation of the curriculum. The curriculum was designed for adults and aimed at empowering learners and transforming their communities. The team that developed the curriculum integrated interactive facilitation practices into its pedagogy and drew from experiences of learners to create a curriculum offered in local languages that included problem-solving, health, literacy, and management.[6]

This curriculum opened the possibility for women to articulate their health concerns in village meetings and to the press. Participants responded to the modules of the curriculum in an unexpected way: they linked their new knowledge to community organization and social action. As a result, they reached out to others in their community and they collectively abandoned the centuries-old practice of female genital cutting (FGC). Other women organized peaceful marches against violence against women and children and/or forced marriage.

This is an example of transformation achieved through a non-formal educational system. Formal education inherited from Europe may not reach such an important audience of the society. Yet, in Africa, it is said that when a woman is educated, the whole community is educated. Women are generally the ones who inculcate social and moral values in young children. They are also the ones who, generally speaking, deal with farming, raising cattle and doing small business to support the family. Furthermore, research in developing countries indicates that a mother's education, especially at the secondary level and above, is more important than a father's education for increasing school enrollment and daughters' higher education because

---

4. See Gillespie and Melching, "Transformative Power of Democracy."
5. Ibid., 484.
6. Ibid., 478.

educated mothers have the bargaining power to direct household resources into their children's, especially their daughters,' educations.[7] Yet, European education may not even be equipped pedagogically to produce transformation that non-formal African education produced in the lives of the learners and their communities.

As Orr puts it, we (Africans) "must not assume that it is education that will save us, or advance us or progress us; rather it is education of a certain kind."[8] Olukoshi and Zeleza suggest that in this twenty-first century Africa needs universities that

> are anchored on the evolution of a knowledge society that it at once rooted in the African context, responding to the needs of the local environment whilst simultaneously engaging with the rest of the world in line with the ideal of the university as an international center for the advancement of science and scholarship.[9]

As I have explained elsewhere, philosophically, Africa needs an education with roots in African values and worldview.[10] Psychologically, this education should touch the cognitive life of the learner as well as his or her affective and volitional life. It should equip the learner with knowledge, transform his or her emotions, prepare the person to make the right decisions and equip one with skills to transform his or her society. Methodologically, this education should be geared toward critical and creative thinking. The curriculum for such an education should be integrative in its design. It should put the spiritual, moral, social, physical, and environmental elements together. It should integrate different methods and should use both formal and non-formal educational models. This is education for holistic transformation.

RATIONALE FOR A STUDY ON EDUCATION FOR HOLISTIC TRANSFORMATION IN AFRICA

Why do we Africans need "education of a certain kind" as Orr puts it?[11] Research indicates that both in the Christian and secular educational milieu,

---

7. See Kazeem et al., "School Attendance in Nigeria."
8. See Orr, "What Is Education For?"
9. Zeleza and Olukoshi, *African Universities in the Twenty-First Century*, 617.
10. See Ntamushobora, "Toward an Understanding."
11. See Orr, "What Is Education For?"

there is concern about ineffectiveness of university graduates. The reasons that are advanced are lack of proper teaching and learning methods that can lead to transformation, but there is also the issue of colonial education that did not reach the goal of transformation in the lives of the learners. Mungazi explains that the British colony, for example, gave itself more power to control the character of African education in such a manner that it produced cheap laborers.[12]

In an article on pedagogical issues in education in Kenya, Ochieng laments that classroom teaching strategies which mainly utilize lecture and demonstration methods are authoritarian methods of lesson delivery in which teachers dictate knowledge to the passive and subdued learners.[13] Ochieng's lament is supported by Kingsbury's statement which points out the general trends of Christian higher education in East Africa:

> Much of the curriculum is irrelevant and non-contextual . . . Learners are often considered empty containers to be filled with deposits from tutors' lectures. What is important for students to learn has been predetermined without their participation. Learners must memorize vast amounts of information to pass exams . . . Transformative learning is unknown.[14]

The implication of Ochieng and Kingsbury's descriptions of education in East Africa in particular, and Africa in general, is that it is more of transmission than transformation. Unfortunately, such a mode of education cannot prepare African graduates to face the challenges and force of today's globalization which "requires innovation, creative, high quality and relevant education, training, research and development" as Ouma and Gravenir put it.[15] It also requires "a continuous reframing of human experiences in order to help individuals and communities in becoming increasingly aware and reflective as well as in developing, negotiating, and sharing new understandings of the world's conditions for better human living and development," as Striano puts it.[16]

This study is important for Christian higher learning given the role that the church is called to play today as the church in Africa experiences exponential growth. However, this growth comes with the following challenges.

12. Mungazi, *Colonial Education for Africans*, 11.
13. Ochieng, "Pedagogical Issues in Education in Kenya."
14. Kingsbury, "Barriers and Facilitators to Teaching," 1.
15. Ouma and Gravenir, "Globalization," 12.
16. Striano, "Managing Educational Transformation," 388.

First, there is imbalance between numerical and spiritual growth in the church. There are many Christian believers in churches in Africa but few of them are transformed in the renewal of their minds (Rom 12:1–2). This explains Guthrie's question after the 1994 genocide in Rwanda, "How do we explain such a bile in a land where, according to the 1991 census, 80 percent of the 8.2 million people are Catholic or Protestant?"[17] This imbalance is caused by a lack of trained leaders who can teach the transforming Word of God, the use of a borrowed curriculum that is not relevant to the need of Africans, and training methods that encourage head knowledge without necessarily changing the heart.

Second, the continent of Africa is facing overwhelming poverty. This poverty is more tragic when we consider that Africa is blessed with natural resources (good land which could make Africa a bread basket for the world); mineral resources (radium in the Democratic Republic of Congo; copper in Zambia; massive reserves of petroleum in Libya; three quarters of the world's gold is in Africa, etc.); energy resources (Africa owns 40 percent of the world's hydropower potential). Africa is suffering from poverty, not because she has no resources, but because, for several reasons (one of them being poor educational systems), Africans have not been able to transform these resources into finished products. Commenting on the contrast between African resources and the prevailing poverty, Adeyemo lamented:

> It is said that Africa is the richest of the seven continents in natural resources and yet people are the poorest. Africa is probably the first home of the human race and yet it is the last to be developed. Africa and Africans have made many nations and people great, yet their own vineyards remain unkempt. How do you explain such set of contradictions?[18]

One of the solutions to the above challenge is an education that can transform Africans holistically and empower them for deliberate engagement in the transformation of their communities into viable places to live.

In addition to the particular problems that the church in Africa is encountering given her strategic place in today's world, both the church and government should work together to face the socio-economic problems that are affecting our communities. One of the examples of these challenges is the stagnant or regressive economy that Africa is experiencing. In March 2005, stakeholders of the World Bank recognized, as Van de Walle had noted

---

17. Guthrie, "Rwanda," 414.
18. Adeyemo, "Africa's Enigma," 31.

The Need for Education for Holistic Transformation in Africa

several years earlier, that "at the beginning of the twenty-first century the African region continues to be outperformed by all other regions, and that efforts to redress this poor performance during the last twenty years has not been successful."[19] Despite billions of dollars that have been poured into Africa, the continent continues to remain poor. Close to 50 percent of the population in Africa is said to live below the poverty line.[20] Adam Szirmai further noted that Africa has the lowest life expectancy in the world. In the year 2000, the average life expectancy in Africa was 51.4 years, compared to South Asia which was 61.5 years.[21] One of the explanations for the persistence of poverty in Africa is the educational curriculum that has been taught in schools across the continent which has been ineffective to transform Africans and to give them their due dignity and freedom of mind and spirit, nor has it equipped them with skills for the transformation of their society. Some of the reasons for this inadequacy are mainly due to the foreign nature of the curriculum to the African culture, and also the substandard quality compared to the Europeans' education as seen earlier.[22] Mungazi wrote an entire book whose thesis was that the British education in Zimbabwe had a negative effect on the educational development of Africans because the colonizers sought to train Africans to serve the interests of the colonial government and that this kind of education left a legacy of educational underdevelopment with which post-colonial Zimbabwe is now wrestling.[23]

A study on education for holistic transformation offers the following advantages: First, the study embraces transformative learning from a holistic perspective including the cognitive, spiritual, relational/affective and communal dimensions. Cognitively speaking, the formal educational systems that Africa inherited from Europe used memorization methodology, and did not prepare learners to be critical thinkers. Kwabena, speaking about the British and curriculum development in West Africa, states, "The way colonial school teachers forced West Africans to memorize information sent the message that rote learning was effective; memorization gave students little opportunity to make meaning of information, and therefore most lacked critical thinking skills."[24] Freire calls this kind of education

19. Van de Walle, *African Economies*, 5.
20. Musyoki, "Social Indicators," 48.
21. Szirmai, *Dynamic of Socio-Economic Development*, 182–83.
22. Kelly, *French Colonial Education*.
23. Mungazi, *Colonial Education*.
24. Kwabena, "British Curriculum Development," 420.

"banking" because it comes as an act of depositing information into the student.[25] Africans need an education that can challenge their underlying assumptions and empower them to explore new perspectives in their lives. This is so important especially in today's need for training university graduates capable of tackling challenges that come with the forces of globalization.

Second, the study acknowledges that an education for head-knowledge is not enough for Africans to be fully transformed. It is a reality that intellectual development does not necessarily guarantee a person the ability to live and practice what is right before God and before men. Dirkx is right when he suggests transformative learning to be about "inviting the person in fullness of being, including an affective, intuitive, thinking, physical and spiritual self."[26] This study therefore promotes an education that can foster a Christ-centered worldview in the lives of people so that they may shine in the current rapidly changing world and take it captive for the Lord of the universe.

Third, the study explores what Africans think about social transformation. While educationists such as Freire and others believe that the outcome of transformative learning should be social change,[27] Africans need to define for themselves what social change means and how institutions of higher learning can be change agents in their contexts. In this way, these institutions would be preparing graduates to do compassionate service in their communities. A research study conducted by Starcher about contextual concerns with respect to a non-Western doctoral program in theology for Africans in Africa revealed that Africans viewed the church as benefiting society because the church was viewed as an instrument of social transformation, not merely as a venue for individual spiritual growth.[28] Africa needs institutions of higher learning that can partner with local communities to bring about positive change in these communities.

In addition to gaining an understanding of education for holistic transformation by instructors and students in institutions of higher learning in Kenya, therefore adding new knowledge to the transformative learning theory in Kenyan context, the findings of this study will be used as a springboard to bring a paradigm shift in education in Sub-Sahara Africa.

25. Freire, *Pedagogy of the Oppressed*, 58.
26. Dirkx, "Engaging Emotions," 22.
27. See Freire, *Pedagogy of the Oppressed*.
28. See Starcher, "Non-Western Doctoral Program."

The Need for Education for Holistic Transformation in Africa

The study draws its data from Kenya, a country in the Sub-Sahara Africa region. This region is the most inhabited; the richest region in terms of natural resources; the most populated with Christians; but, unfortunately, one of the poorest regions in the world.[29] Changing Sub-Saharan Africa is, generally speaking, changing Africa at large. Also, Kenya is strategic because professors and students in both Christian and secular institutions of higher learning come from all over Africa. The findings of this study will therefore give some hints as to what education for holistic transformation could look like in other parts of Africa.

The third significance of the study is that it will yield credible findings in the area of transformative learning in the African context. The study will draw its data from African scholars who understand the topic and live the reality discussed. They have solid suggestions to make about the research study. It is, therefore, expected that the finding of this study will constitute a grounded theory that will promote and support further research.

The fourth significance of the study is that it will serve as an inspiration to the disciplines that are using the same terms of holistic transformation without prior empirical research, such as missions, community development, theology, and others. This study will be foundational to further research not only for the field of education but also for other related disciplines.

Finally, the study will ultimately challenge African educators in their views about transformative learning in a holistic dimension. They will understand the role of such a new paradigm in leadership development and curriculum change for the education of the generation of young African scholars and community leaders during this era of globalization.

---

29. See Van der Walt, "Challenge of Christian Higher Education."

2

Brief History of Education in Africa

For education to be effective, it needs to be relevant to and consistent with the needs, values, context and goals of a society. The context of a society should be the standard of judgment for the effectiveness of education, for the goal of education is to empower people to be able to transform their society. That is why it would not be appropriate to speak about transformative learning before we understand learning in the African context. This calls us to consider learning as it took place in the traditional African society, during colonial times and after independence. The study of the context of education in Africa will therefore lay a foundation for an understanding of the need for holistic transformation in Africa, how the past has contributed to either the failure or success of this form of learning, and the gap that needs to be closed.

EDUCATION IN TRADITIONAL AFRICA

Fafunwa, Sifuna, Adeyemi and Adeyinka, and Lewis explain the goals, contents, methods and philosophy of traditional African education.[1] The writers point out that many years before the coming of the Europeans on the African continent there was an effective education system in each African clan, tribe or kingdom. African traditional education was effective,

---

1. See Fafunwa and Aisiku, *Education in Africa*; Sifuna, *Development of Education in Africa*; Adeyemi and Adeyinka, "Principles and Content of African Traditional Education"; and Lewis, *Education in Africa*.

tangible, definite and clearly intelligible, as opposed to the views of some who think that Africans never taught their young people. Indigenous education was essentially an education for life. Its main purpose was to train the youth for adulthood within society. Emphasis was put on normative and expressive goals which were concerned with accepted standards and beliefs governing correct behavior. Expressive goals were concerned with unity and consensus. This is an indication that education in traditional Africa encouraged democracy as opposed to some who think that traditional Africa did not know about democracy.

In its various forms, traditional education had a many-sided character intimately intertwined with social life. This is another confirmation that Africans understood what integration was all about. To make this education relevant, what was taught was related to the social context in which people were called to live. This education was not only concerned with the systematic socialization of the younger generation into norms, beliefs and collective opinions of the wider society, but it also placed a very strong emphasis on learning practical skills and the acquisition of knowledge which was useful to the individual and society as a whole. So, transformation did not concern only the individual but also the society at large. This is the reason why I am advocating for "holistic transformation," instead of just "transformation."

The curriculum of this education was drawn from the real environment. From the physical environment children had to learn about weather, landscapes and animal and insect life. The economic role of the children featured prominently in their training. Parents and older relatives were responsible for the training in economic responsibilities, and learning by imitation played an important role as the smaller children followed the example of the older in building, herding or hunting, in the case of boys, or sweeping, carrying wood and water, or cooking for girls. Religious education was important for education in traditional Africa. Religion, which was concerned with morality, gave support to the laws and customs of the community and to its accepted rules of conduct which included courtesy, generosity and honesty. Traditional educators applied various methods of instruction. Contrary to the thoughts that attribute formal education to European education, traditional African education used both formal and informal methods. Among the informal methods of instruction were learning through play, engaging in make-believe play activities which were initiative, imaginative and symbolic, and wrestling. Other play activities included swinging, chasing one another aimlessly, sliding and dances performed in moonlight after evening meals. Oral literature constituted an important method of instruction. This included teaching through myths and legends. Much of ethical teachings were given to children through folktales, most of which had happy endings and involved triumph over difficulties. Virtues such as communal unity, hard work, conformity, honesty and uprightness were reflected in many of the folktales. Children also learnt through dance and folk songs and proverbs.

Formal methods of instruction involved theoretical and practical inculcation of skills. Learning through apprenticeship, for example, was formal and direct. Parents who wanted their children to acquire some occupational training normally sent them to work with craftsmen such as potters, blacksmiths and basket-makers. These could be called non-formal methods today because of the comparison with the formal methods which give credentials, but in the case of African traditional education that was formal education. African traditional education was based on the following philosophical principles: preparationism (boys and girls were equipped with the skills appropriate to their gender in preparation for their distinctive roles in the society); functionalism (education was utilitarian as an immediate induction into society and a preparation for adulthood); communalism (all members of the society owned things in common and applied the communal spirit to life and work); perennialism (used as a vehicle for maintaining and preserving the cultural heritage and status quo); and wholisticism (aims, contents and methods were inextricably interwoven, and so the holistic approach to learning developed children into jacks-of-all-trades and masters of all).

Adeyemi and Adeyinka discussed two major weaknesses of the African traditional education.[2] The first is that it mainly focused on clan or tribe, along with its oral rather than its written literacy thereby restricting the transfer of skills and knowledge across space and time. A second general weakness was that the traditional African education favored indoctrination rather than reflective thinking. The first element of the above critiques has some validity but its degree of reliability is low. Education was not done only within a clan. Young boys and girls would travel for long distances to be mentored or go through apprenticeship within another clan or tribe. That was acceptable. It is true that oral communication limited the transfer of skills and training, but it also encouraged the use of memory in educa-

---

2. See Adeyemi and Adeyinka, "Principles and Content."

tion. I rather agree with the second critique because the teacher-mentor had authority over the learner-protégé and the learner was generally to follow the instruction of the mentor without much questioning. This is the reason why I am advocating for symbiosis between the Western formal education and the traditional African education system as a system that could lead to holistic transformation in Africa in this twenty-first century.

As one can observe, education in traditional Africa was adapted to the cultural setting of the time. First, the communal way of life was a school in itself. People shared a feeling of belonging, solidarity and cooperation. It was in this kind of environment that education took place. This promoted character development which is important for human development, and which was eroded by the individualistic form of education that was introduced later by missionaries and colonialists.

Also, education in traditional Africa was integrated. Learning took place in daily life, and the acquisition of knowledge went along with the acquisition of skills and character development. As Lewis argues, although the Europeans labeled education in traditional Africa as "backward," maybe because it was different from theirs, it was fit for the needs of the African society of that time.[3]

It is hard to predict how traditional education would have evolved if Africa had not had contact with the formal European educational system. Perhaps the West would have had more things to learn from Africa than today. Today, Africans are in psychological ambivalence where education is concerned. Africans who go to school in formal systems tend to lose their traditional values. At the same time, even if they go through Western educational systems they do not become Western. Abidogun, illustrating this ambivalence as experienced in Nigeria, points out that today it would be difficult to define what is Northern Igbo culture in Nigeria, and it would also be difficult to accurately discern what parts of its cosmology are indigenous and what developed in response to European incursions into this area of Nigeria.[4] The challenge of education in Africa is to have a system that allows Africans to keep their identity and at the same time understand and cope with the challenges of globalization.

The following section deals with education in Africa during the colonial period. The section explores the colonial educational policy, focusing on the French and British educational systems.

3 Lewis, *Education in Africa*.
4. See Abidogun, "Western Education's Impact."

EDUCATION IN AFRICAN COLONIAL PERIOD

European colonization that divided Africa into colonies at the end of the nineteenth century (1885) lasted about a century. Africa was colonized by Britain, France, Belgium and Portugal, but the first two European countries were the main colonizers.

Missionaries played a key role in the education of Africans. As Kwabena puts it, the philosophy that guided colonial missionary education and its curriculum was evangelistic.[5] Consequently, given that African forms of religion or worship were not an entry point to the kingdom of God (considered to be based on animism, witchcraft, paganism, and superstition rather than the Bible), African forms of spirituality, including music, dancing, art, and religious practices were all excluded from the colonial curriculum. He also asserts that there was a strong urge in colonial curriculum planners to enrich the curriculum with contents that would lead Africans on the path of civility and modernization. Quoting Taylor, the author points out that missionaries were motivated by their desire to give rather than to take, and to offer what they believed to be the best form of their own culture.[6] Given that Europe was making modern progress at that time, missionaries saw it as their religious duty to share these "modern" happenings with their African brothers and sisters through an evangelizing and civilizing mission.

To make these social transformations possible, the missionaries turned to the educational system, and Africans who attended mission schools were required to adopt European dress, culture, language, and values.[7] For instance, when the British took charge of Ghana, Sierra Leone, Gambia and Nigeria during the later part of the nineteenth century, British educational planners designed and implemented curricula for West African schools that followed the European model. The content of the curriculum in all public schools changed to focus more on British topics, concepts, and interests. The missionaries, however, made a significant attempt to use local languages in their schools and translated the Bible into local languages during the latter half of the nineteenth century.

Kwabena spells out the consequences of this foreign curriculum.[8] First, the contents of its lessons introduced pupils to a new lifestyle. One

---

5. See Kwabena, "British Curriculum Development."
6. See Taylor, "Missionary Education in Africa Reconsidered."
7. See Brummett, *Civilization*.
8. See Kwabena, "British Curriculum Development."

of the consequences of this change of lifestyle was the fact that children who followed this type of curriculum disregarded many important Western African customs. Methodologically, the curriculum emphasized "bookwork" over "handwork" and therefore gave an erroneous impression that schooling was designed to produce clerks, teachers, and missionaries. Also, a rigid bureaucratic school administration drove most students to adopt harmful habits such as indiscipline, deceit, and insubordination. Third, the practice of missionaries of renaming Africans undermined African identity and personality and brought about a new generation of Africans who saw themselves as having the mind of Europeans and consequently, repudiated the traditional African way of life. Finally, the way colonial school teachers forced West Africans to memorize information sent the message that rote learning was effective. Memorization gave little opportunity to make meaning of information, and therefore most of them lacked critical thinking skills.

Kelly provides an analysis of the French colonial educational policy and practice in West Africa.[9] The book presents the French colonial educational policy, educational practice, and the reaction of the colonized to these policies and practices in the two major areas of French colonial domination during the nineteenth and twentieth centuries—that is, Vietnam and West Africa. The latter constitutes our interest. Kelly points out that "school texts taught in French colonial Africa contributed to the development of a distinct cultural milieu in the classroom."[10] The texts pointed out that despite their education, schooled Africans were still only blacks and would remain so even if they came to possess the accoutrements of French lifestyles and culture. The colonial powers were mainly interested in maintaining order and stability. To do this, they needed only some members of the local population educated to assist with the operation of the colonial establishment. The French were careful to keep the numbers low, both to save money and to ensure that not too many were exposed to subversive Western ideas.

As Kelly argues, the education provided by the French in the colonies was far from equal to that provided at home.[11] The French tried to design their schooling to ensure loyalty and subservience, and tried not to overeducate the indigenous population. Only a tiny fraction could obtain an education, and the schooling that they did receive was far inferior to that

---

9. Kelly, *French Colonial Education*.
10. Ibid., 191.
11. Ibid.

provided in France. When indigenous people struck out on their own and established their own schools, the French feared insurrection and shut the schools down.

From the reading about education in both the British and French colonial systems, there are four causes among many others that may have been the source of a lack of effectiveness of the colonial educational system in Africa.

First of all, the curriculum that was taught in Africa during the colonial time was not relevant to the need of Africans. For instance, in 1903 at Livingstonia Mission in northern Malawi, a standard-five examination paper asked pupils "to explain the claim of King James VI to the English Crown" and "to describe the shortest sea route from Glasgow to Inverness."[12] Unfortunately, even today not much has been done to adapt the curriculum to the needs of time and people. Bassey points out, "Education in Africa is still designed after Western models and paradigms that are not connected to life as it is in Africa."[13] He goes further: "African institutions, particularly African universities, still teach economics, political science, sociology, philosophy, geography, science, and so forth, as they are taught in Europe and America and with books imported from Europe and America."[14] No wonder, graduates of such institutions are not able to be connected to the life of the community! Bassey then is right when he states, "What is taught in Africa has no direct relevance to the needs and circumstances of the people of Africa."[15]

Second, when Western education was introduced to Africa, colonizers did not consider the traditional African educational system to be relevant. The aim of education became to earn status and credentials instead of bringing transformation in the life of the learner. Fafunwa gives the following seven aspects of traditional African education which made it holistic:

> First, to develop the child's latent physical skills; second, to develop character; third, to inculcate respect for elders and those in positions of authority; fourth, to develop intellectual skills; fifth, to acquire specific vocational training and to develop a healthy attitude toward honest labor; sixth, to develop a sense of belonging and to encourage active participation in family and community

---

12. McCracken, "Livingstonia in the Development of Malawi."
13. Bassey, *Western Education and Political Domination*, 47.
14. Ibid.
15. Ibid.

affairs; finally, to understand, appreciate and promote cultural heritage of the community at large.[16]

Third, although missionaries had a passion to train African leaders, they trained the elite that would govern the masses, and by doing so, they created classes instead of empowered communities. Ward gives the example of "protestant high schools such as Trinity College, Achemota (Gold Coast—today Ghana), King's College Budo (Uganda), the Alliance High School (Kenya) which trained the political leaders who were to lead British African colonies into independence."[17] Unfortunately, as Bassey explains, because of the gap between those political leaders and the illiterate population, most of the leaders became dictators over their own people, and were manipulated by the colonial powers which still wanted to extend their influence and dominance over political and economic matters in Africa.[18]

In addition, missionaries who trained leaders for the rural areas did so by choosing those with a peasant background to serve the rural base of the mission. Unfortunately, as Ward concludes, "This training could not empower newly trained leaders to replace the missionaries when they left after independence in the 1960s."[19]

However, Adeyemo and Baur appreciate the effort of the early missionaries in building schools and hospitals.[20] It therefore seems that, although the missionaries had an agenda in limiting education to a small number of elites, as Bassey points out,[21] those who were educated and became oppressors of their compatriots should receive the blame rather than the missionaries. This statement could be supported by the remark by Milton Obote, former president of Uganda, who stated, "Had it not been for the revolutionary teaching of the Church concerning justice, Uganda would not have achieved its independence."[22] Obote acknowledged the good work of the church prior to independence, unfortunately most of African leaders after independence became corrupt and dictators.

---

16. Fafunwa and Aisiku, *Education in Africa*, 11–12.
17. Ward, "Christianity, Colonialism and Missions," 78.
18. Bassey, *Western Education and Political Domination*.
19. Ward, "Christianity, Colonialism and Missions," 81.
20. See Adeyemo, *African Contribution to Christendom*; Baur, *2000 Years of Christianity*.
21. Bassey, *Western Education and Political Domination*.
22. Byaruhanga, *Bishop Alfred Robert Tucker*, 31.

Fourth, colonizers and missionaries used Western educational methods that did not fit the African worldview. Education was more cognitive than relationship oriented. In the Western educational system, learning takes place by reading books while in the traditional African educational system, learning took place by interacting with age-mates, elders who are wise, and others. Comparing the traditional Kikuyu system in Kenya with the European system, Kenyatta once observed:

> The striking thing in Kikuyu system of education and the feature which most sharply distinguishes it from the European system of education is the primary place given to personal relations. Each official statement of educational policy repeats this well-worn declaration that the aim of education must be building of character and not the mere acquisition of knowledge, but the European practice falls short of this principle. While the Westerner asserts that character formation is the chief thing, he forgets that character is formed primarily through relations with other people, and that there is really no other way in which it can grow.[23]

Regarding the church, lack of trained leaders and illiteracy affected discipleship. Despite the mushrooming of churches in Africa today, there are many churches that are led by illiterate leaders, non-trained pastors, or several churches operating under one pastor. All these are conditions that hindered believers from transformation in their lives.

What can we learn about education during the period that followed independence? What are the challenges that education went through in the young independent African nations? Are these challenges over today? These are the questions that are examined in the following section of education in postcolonial Africa.

EDUCATION IN POSTCOLONIAL AFRICA

This section discusses the challenges of education during the postcolonial time. Empirical studies are analyzed to support the arguments developed. These challenges explain the need for a new type of education—holistic transformation. The challenges that are considered are socio-cultural, relevance, economic, professional and methodological.

---

23. Kenyatta, *Facing Mount Kenya*, 121.

Brief History of Education in Africa

Socio-Cultural Challenges of Education in Postcolonial Africa

Education in postcolonial Africa which, generally speaking, is the continuation of the colonial form of education poses some socio-cultural challenges to learners. This form of education makes learners lose access to indigenous knowledge, separates the learners from their cultural practices even when these practices would have been beneficial to the learner and his or her society and promotes an individualistic attitude among the learners, thus making them less human. From an African ontological perspective, to be human is to have a sense of *Ubuntu*—the humanness acquired in community belonging.

Abidogun conducted a study that analyzed gender perspective at two secondary schools in Nsukka, a region inhabited by the Igbo people of Nigeria. The study sought to identify the impact of formal education on indigenous gender roles. The study discusses their loss of indigenous knowledge, changes in marriage and family roles, the marginalization of female political roles, and an increased status of formal education that places a premium on male education. The questions in the research were designed to elicit cross-generational information based on student knowledge of themselves, their peers, their parents, and their grandparents, as well as their general knowledge of Northern Igbo culture. Open-ended interviews were used to elicit information about students' knowledge of their lineages and histories.

The finding revealed that formal education had influence on a loss of indigenous knowledge. All students reported a loss of or nonparticipation in particular social practices, traditional occupations and craft, or skills that required indigenous knowledge (here, indigenous knowledge is identified as information or learning that was expected to be attained through indigenous education practices, such as age-grade training and mentoring by gender, and apprenticeship within the Northern Igbo community structure). Many students stated, "I believe that if I don't achieve anything in [formal] education I will not be someone in the future." This statement showed that formal education was replacing indigenous education as the preferred or necessary education system. Students reported that even those who were trained in traditional skills lost this knowledge because they stopped participating due to the physical separation from the community to attend secondary school, its increased demands, and their changed social status as an "educated" person.[24] Many of the girls reported

---

24. Abidogun, "Western Education's Impact," 34.

that they could not process palm oil, or did not know traditional dances that their non-formally educated peers knew. Many of the boys indicated that they did not know how to hunt, farm or fish as well as their non-formally educated peers. Overall, students indicated limited participation or non-participation in Northern Igbo festivals and ceremonies. The usual reason they gave for non-participation was that these activities were part of traditional religion.

Some of the influences of the formal education on family and marriage include the fact that the Igbo cultural norm of keeping boys and girls socially segregated until they were married had changed. Formal education supported social interaction between boys and girls through mixed classes and shared common space at school that replicated Western education practices. Also, the ability to interact socially through formal education contributed to a decrease in polygamous and arranged marriages and weakened the extended family's role within marriage.

Finally, significantly these students demonstrated a lack of knowledge of the Igbo dual sex political system. Students could not identify the groups that Achebe describes as *umuada* ("daughters of the lineage") and *ndiaomu* ("wives of the village") who often "combined forces in a Women's Assembly." This decreased knowledge and participation was a direct result of the kind of Judeo-Christian doctrine taught in the schools and in local churches.

In the conclusion, Abidogun suggested that Northern Igbo education leaders should review and reassess the curriculum and students' circumstances to evaluate how more indigenous knowledge could be incorporated into the system.

In another research, Kazeem, Jensen and C. Stokes were interested in discovering how gender, urban-rural residence, and socio-economic status bear on children's school attendance in particular contexts.[25] The study was based on two hypotheses: First, boys are more likely than girls to attend school. Second, the penalty of being a girl who attends school is greater among poor households. The research posited that both economic and cultural factors were important in Nigeria for six reasons. First, the country is a male-dominated society, with cultural beliefs that promote the social, economic, and educational advancement of males over females. Second, research in Sub-Sahara Africa has found that children of Christian parents have more years of schooling than children with Muslim parents. Third,

---

25. See Kazeem et al., "School Attendance in Nigeria."

traditional African religions endorse the preparation of girls for domestic roles, and they are taught these roles through play and informal education. Fourth, research has found that children who live in urban areas have higher levels of schooling than children in rural areas. Fifth, research in developing countries shows that parents' education has a positive relationship with their children's education. Sixth, research in developing countries also indicate that a mother's education, especially at the secondary level and above, is more important than a father's education for increasing school enrollment and years of education of daughters because educated mothers have the bargaining power to direct household resources into their children's, especially their daughters,' education.

Results of the study indicated a clear gender gap in current school attendance among Nigerian children, whereby male children are consistently more likely to be attending school. The same finding indicated that other things being equal, the odds of attending school are 84 percent greater for boys than for girls. Also, the same study indicated that children whose mothers have at least some primary education are significantly more likely to attend school than children whose mothers have no education, and the effects increase monotonically with mother's education. At the extreme, children whose mothers completed secondary or higher education are over fourteen times more likely to attend school than those whose mothers have no education. Father's education showed similar but weaker effects on school attendance. The difference in magnitude for mother's and father's education suggested that, in the Nigerian context, mother's education had a particularly strong effect on children's current school attendance. Also, results from the study indicated that Christian children were five times more likely to attend school than Muslim children. Even children of traditional and other religions were twice as likely as Muslim children to attend. The research suggested that given the challenge in increasing school enrollment rates and eliminating gender and socio-economic disparities in school attendance, policies and programs should focus on socio-economic factors retarding the schooling of children from lower socio-economic segments of the population.

In addition to socio-cultural challenges of education in post-colonial Africa, research has shown that there are also challenges related to relevance of education in the newly independent African nations.

Education for Holistic Transformation in Africa

Challenges of Relevance of Education in Postcolonial Africa

The problem of relevance of education in postcolonial Africa is a cry in both secular and religious education in Africa. Public schools and theological institutions in Africa continue to use curriculums that are imported from the West, therefore rendering learning irrelevant to the needs of the learners and his or her community.

Adekunle, in his article "Decolonizing Theological Education in Nigeria," deplores the fact that theological education in Nigeria has failed to achieve the envisaged objective of holistic transformation. Though Christianity has spread widely in Nigeria, it is without roots in the lives of the people. The author points out that one of the factors that accounts for the under-performance of theological education in Nigeria is that it is rooted in the colonial context. According to Adekunle, the early indigenous Christian leaders had a training that detached them from their socio-cultural milieu.[26] Imasogie is quoted by Adekunle explaining the consequence of such a detached training:

> The approach has tended to require the African to pledge a superficial allegiance to the "stranger-God" of the Whiteman who, in his thinking, does not understand his situation. He accepts this God only intellectually, thus giving the false impression that he thereby denies the God whom he existentially recognizes as the foundation of his traditional beliefs and practices. Since old habits die hard, especially in the absence of an existential commitment to a new mode of self-understanding, it is easy to understand why the pull to the old and familiar triumphs when crisis strikes.[27]

In the second part of his article, Adekunle speaks about decolonization of theological education in Nigeria. The author suggests that theological education in Nigeria should be rooted in the traditional cultural values, which create indigenous awareness.[28] However, the author considers Oladipo's advice that "the relationship between the African theologian and his/her cultural heritage should not be one of uncritical acceptance or total opposition to what can be construed as its central elements."[29] According to the author, "Proper relationship should be one of constructive engage-

---

26. See Adekunle, "Decolonizing Theological Education."
27. Imasogie, *Guidelines for Christian Theology*, 149.
28. Adekunle, "Decolonizing Theological Education," 154.
29. Ibid., 155; referencing Oladipo, introduction to *Third Way*.

Brief History of Education in Africa

ment, in which the task of exposition, analysis, criticism and reconstruction go together."[30] Second, Adekunle suggests that theological education in Nigeria must be holistic in character.[31] Theological education should not be compartmentalized into sacred and secular, and should avoid the mind-body or affective-cognitive dualism. Pedagogically, Adekunle suggests the use of local languages or vernacular in theological education.[32] He quotes Clarke when he says:

> Only a reflection of the experience of Christ in the vernacular can create the kind of theological consciousness that is genuinely African. In the meantime much of the theological activity in Christian Africa remains within the oral matrix from the living experience of the people who hear the word of God in their own tongue and respond to it through song, dance, preaching and prayer.[33]

To further illustrate the challenge of relevance, Wolhuter and Steyn carried out an investigation to compare the education system in Madagascar and that in South Africa.[34] Research was done by means of field observations as well as discussions and interviews with role players at regional education offices and schools.

The study led to the conclusion that neither of the educational systems was sufficiently adapted to the real education needs and real situation in the respective countries. In both countries, the tendency was to simulate, to some extent, the education systems and education practices of the previous colonial governments—namely, France and Britain. In so doing, learners were not provided with the opportunity to equip themselves with the required competences to function effectively according to their real education needs.

In another study, Ansell explains the problem of relevance of education in Africa.[35] The study is an analysis of the educational needs of rural girls in Lesotho and Zimbabwe in the current form of secondary education. The author acknowledges that since the two countries gained independence from colonial rule they have continued to use the colonial-style curricula and to focus on public examinations. Yes, these practices do little

---

30. Adekunle, "Decolonizing Theological Education," 155.
31. Ibid.
32. Ibid.
33. Clarke, "In Our Mother Tongue," 159.
34. See Wolhuter and Steyn, "Learning from South-South Comparison."
35. See Ansell, "Secondary Education Reform."

to fulfill the needs of rural girls in either country. The study indicates that although the two countries expanded their number of secondary schools, graduates from these schools are not employed. For instance, in 1981, a year after Zimbabwe obtained independence, 463 new secondary schools opened. By 1989 the secondary Gross Enrollment Ratio of 45% was among the highest in Africa. Yet, in Zimbabwe over 300,000 young people leave school every year, but only 15,000 to 30,000 new jobs are created. The author explains that this is due to the fact that the focus of schools is upon examinations, which restricts other aspects of education that might be of more value to young people. Lessons tend to be geared towards memorization of the "facts" that are tested in examinations. There is little concern with the development of higher order cognitive skills, little encouragement to be creative or to challenge/critique received knowledge.

Regarding employment for females, the author explains that in both countries male labor migration has left rural population dominated by women. In Zimbabwe, for example, enrollment in secondary school is considerably lower among girls than among boys, and examination pass rates are also lower. In Lesotho, by contrast, girls outnumber boys in schools, a situation almost unique in Africa, but one that has a long history. In both Zimbabwe and Lesotho, rural women are said to perform a triple role, engaging in production, household reproduction and community management. Yet secondary curricula remain, as in colonial times, largely irrelevant to rural girls. Few of the academic subject studies are of direct use in the performance of rural women's triple roles. The author concludes that there is a glaring need for consideration of gender in education to go beyond concern for numbers and pass rates, for success in these areas is insufficient to meet girls' educational needs, without attention to the type of education provided.

Explaining why vocational training is not a priority in these two countries, the author points out that vocational training was considered inferior by colonialists themselves and only provided to those deemed insufficiently able intellectually. Also, black children always received more vocational education in school than white children. Third, academic education generally led to better paid employment than vocational training. Finally, even with vocational training, blacks were unable to obtain apprenticeships or skilled jobs as legislation reserved these for whites.

The study concluded that there was an increasingly perceived need to cater to the majority of young people who leave school with no qualification,

Brief History of Education in Africa

and who remain economically inactive. This potential must be acted upon in the interests of rural girls, however. Otherwise the response to these contradictions might simply be a contradiction of secondary education.

In addition to socio-cultural and relevance challenges of education in the post-colonial period, African nations have experienced economic challenges in their educational efforts.

Economic Challenges

Education in postcolonial Africa has gone through economic challenges. This goes with Africa's economy that has been in malaise for several decades, especially beginning in the 1970s. Akilagpa explains that the general decline in conditions, qualifications, and morale at the universities has been exacerbated by a decrease in the incentive packages available to faculty members.[36] The situation became worse with the economic downturns of the 1970s and 1980s. In addition, the exodus of some of the best minds, especially among young and midcareer faculty, and the inability of the universities to recruit or retain qualified replacements in adequate number, have been the inevitable consequences of all these declines. This case is a reality not only in higher education but also in primary and secondary education levels.

In a research, Omotayo, Ihebereme and Maduewesi explain that both the educational system introduced in 1982 in Nigeria known as 6-3-3-4 (six years in primary school, three years in Junior secondary school, another three years in senior secondary school and four years in a tertiary institution) and the Universal Basic Education (UBE) introduced in 1999 have gone through several problems.[37] The first problem was inaccurate data for planning. More often than not educational planning in Nigeria is based on projected statistics data often inaccurate for educational planning. The second problem was inadequate funding which has crippled effective implementation of UBE and the 6-3-3-4 system of education. The third problem was inadequate supply of facilities and equipment. Most of the existing structures are dilapidated and in a state of disrepair, and most school libraries and laboratories are ill equipped. The fourth problem was inadequate supply of competent teachers. The UBE implementation committee estimated that about 1.2 million pupils would be registered for the

36. See Akilagpa, "Challenges Facing African Universities."
37. See Omotayo et al., "Management of Universal Basic Education Scheme."

scheme at a ratio of 1:40 and so, about 84,270 trained teachers would be required to effectively cater to the number of the registered children. The fifth problem was poor monitoring and evaluation. The monitoring and evaluation system under the UBE program was ineffective and was not able to assure quality control in the design and implementation process of UBE. The sixth problem was that the curriculum of the UBE scheme was not directed to meet the emerging socio-economic demands of the twenty-first century through skills acquisition and computer literacy.

Most of the problems affecting education in Nigeria are finance related. Unfortunately, the same problems are reported in other countries in Africa. Lack of sufficient allocation of funds for education contributes to teacher attrition, education of a small proportion of students, inadequate learning conditions and low quality of education.

Other researchers such as Kizito and Ondigi conducted a study whose purpose was to identify, analyze the factors that influence teacher attrition, and to find out how teacher shortage was addressed in the schools.[38] This study was due to the fact that, although African schools produce needed qualified teachers, this does not lead to or result in socio-economic transformation unless and until opportunities are created for their proper utilization, a condition that is lacking in Africa. The study was carried out in Kisumu city of Nyanza province of Western Kenya.

The study found that the 24 schools had 611 teachers in 1998 instead of 660, a shortfall of 49 teachers. By 2002, the year of the study, there were 540 teachers, therefore between 1998 and 2002 there was a shortfall of 161 teachers and the total shortfall had risen to 210, representing 31%. Due to this shortfall of teachers, most teachers in languages and mathematics/science departments were overloaded with over 28 lessons a week unlike their counterparts in humanities and technical/applied departments with less than 28 lessons per week. These extra lessons, therefore, made it difficult for these teachers to plan, organize and teach effectively.

Data from the head teachers' responses indicated that the deficit was caused by teacher attrition (twenty head teachers representing 83.3%) while four responses representing only 16.7% denied that teacher deficit was caused by teacher attrition. Further data analysis revealed that most of the teachers who left the profession had not been replaced hence only 16 schools had received new teachers totaling up to 31 by the year 2002. The main factors that were identified for teacher attrition were alternative

---

38. See Kizito and Ondigi, "Analysis of the Factors."

occupation (70.8%) and further studies (58.3%). This was attributed to low salary and job opportunities available in the civil service and private sector respectively. Teacher attrition bears consequences on learning conditions of students, working conditions of teachers and on quality of education in general.

Also, Wamukuru, Kamau and Ochola explored teacher effectiveness and the challenges that affect Free Primary Education (FPE) and specifically the views of the teachers involved in the implementation of this Universal Primary Education (UPE) initiative of Kenya.[39] The target population for this study included all public primary school teachers in Kenya. A convention sample of 354 teachers undertaking the school-based bachelor of education (primary option) of the Teacher Education Program (TEP) within Ergerton University's College of Distance Education was selected for the study.

The study revealed that teachers perceive the introduction of FPE to have brought with it challenges that are currently affecting their effectiveness. Teacher effectiveness in the management and marking of student classroom exercises and examinations has been greatly hampered with over 65% of the respondents indicating that due to the over-enrollment the difficulty of marking and offering individual remedial work to every student are key obstacles to learning.

In addition, all respondents stated that significant age differences that are now common in public primary school classrooms present special challenges to both teachers and learners. Also, there are gross staffing inadequacies resulting in staff experiencing strain due to the increased workload, over-enrollment, and the government's inability to increase the teaching workforce. About 87% of the respondents indicated that the teaching and learning materials provided by FPE have been adversely affected in primary schools with evident deterioration in their quality, quantity, and effective use. The adequacy of teachers is clearly the most outstanding challenge posed by the introduction of FPE in Kenyan primary schools.

Apart from socio-cultural, relevance and economic challenges that African nations have faced after independence, they have also faced professional challenges in their educational efforts.

---

39. See Wamukuru et al., "Challenge of Implementing Free Primary Education."

Education for Holistic Transformation in Africa

Professional Challenges

Education in Africa is today confronted by insufficient numbers of teachers who are skilled and qualified to help students grow in academics and acquire skills to transform their communities. Some of the reasons for this insufficiency are related to financial limitations of the budget, low salaries, irrelevant curriculum that does not prepare graduates for the task, and the perception that some subjects are only or primarily for males and that arts are only for females.

According to Teferra and Altbach, the most serious challenge facing many African countries is the departure of their best scholars and scientists away from universities.[40] The flow away from domestic academe takes a form of internal mobility (locally) and regional and overseas migration. The internal mobility of scholars can be described as the flow of high level expertise from the universities to better-paying government agencies and private institutions and firms that may or may not utilize their expertise and talent effectively.[41] Also, many academic departments have lost their preeminent faculty members to regional universities in other parts of Africa. For instance, several senior scholars from Addis Ababa University, Ethiopia, hold faculty positions at the University of Botswana. Zambia has also been complaining about the migration of their graduates and academic community to South Africa and Zimbabwe.

As Teferra and Altbach report, a 1998 study shows that in 1990, nearly 7,000 Kenyans with tertiary-level education migrated to the United States. Sethi says that in the same year (1990), nearly 120 doctors were estimated to have emigrated from Ghana.[42] Between 600 and 700 Ghanaian physicians, a number equal to about 50% of the total population of doctors remaining in the country, are known to be practicing in the United States alone. Yet an analysis of existing vacancies in the tertiary institutions in Ghana indicates that about 40% of faculty positions in the universities and more than 60% of those in the polytechnics are vacant. The same migrations take place in many other African countries.

An ethnographic study of 120 migrant teachers, conducted by Manik, revealed that teachers leave South Africa because of career dissatisfaction,

---

40. See Teferra and Altbach, "African Higher Education."
41. Ibid., 41.
42. See Sethi, "Return and Reintegration."

Brief History of Education in Africa

financial and travel incentives, and global grandeur.[43] The same study revealed that some young teachers who migrate to the United Kingdom soon return home because of poor student discipline, climate and loneliness that impacts teacher welfare.

In addition to brain drain, due to poor teacher preparation, education in Africa suffers from a lack of competent teachers. As seen earlier, teaching methods in Africa do not promote critical thinking and reflection. These teachers cannot pass on what they do not have. Their teaching becomes characterized by transmission instead of transformation and their students therefore inherit an uncritical mind and habit.

This is well explained by Lombard and Grosser, who conducted a study in South Africa about critical thinking abilities among prospective educators.[44] The purpose of the study was to elucidate the critical thinking abilities of a group of prospective educators in light of the ideals being put forward by the African Renaissance and the South African Qualifications Authority. In the study, critical thinking was conceived as consisting of induction, deduction, value judgment, definition, observation, identification of assumptions, giving meaning and determining credibility.

It was observed that the majority of respondents tested below the median. The finding revealed that the deficiency with regard to the execution of critical thinking skills was a problem that covered the ethnic, age, gender, and socio-economic variables.

When considering the total sample's average percentage obtained in each of the seven sub-tests of critical thinking, it was obvious that the respondents excelled in none of these. The study recommended that a contextualized research instrument appropriate to South Africa be developed, and that extensive research be done to establish the critical thinking ability of all South African educators. Such a study would be important because if educators are to play a pivotal role in the development of learners' critical thinking skills, they should change their classroom practices and should reflect competence in the ability to think critically.

Also, Miheso discusses the finding of her other research carried out in 2002 on "factors affecting performance in Mathematics among secondary school students."[45] The aim of the study was to identify the extent to which classroom level factors contributed to student performance. The

---

43. See Manik, "To Greener Pastures."
44. See Lombard and Grosser, "Critical Thinking Abilities."
45. Miheso, "Relationship between Interactive Teaching," 73.

performance was measured through achievement tests against cognitive levels. The study was motivated by the large standard deviations that exist in performance of mathematics in the country's annual examinations—Kenya Certificate of Secondary Education (KCSE).

The preliminary statistics indicated that the majority of classes (76.8%) in the sample schools were found to be large with at least 41 students. The small classes, which formed 23.2% of the total sample, had class-sizes ranging from 26 to 38 students. This is relatively large by international standards where a small class size has 20 students.

The research suggested that teachers need to vary their teaching approach and make deliberate efforts to promote higher order thinking skills at the classroom level. Also, contrary to other research findings where women were found to score somewhat lower than men,[46] the findings established the fact that opportunity to learn when appropriated effectively does not discriminate between boys and girls. Their study rather suggested that difference in mathematics achievement between men and women could be explained by differences in background, ability, attitudes, grades, and formal exposure to mathematics in the classroom, but "of these the variables measuring exposure to mathematics had the most influence on explaining variation in mathematics achievement."[47]

In terms of methodology, higher education in Africa has also fallen short of critical thinking ability and competence. According to Kingsbury, existing formal educational systems in East Africa (and Africa at large) do not promote a critically reflective style of thinking or a very transformative and participatory pedagogical mode.[48] As a result, such an education system which is centered on external examinations does not facilitate the type of reflective thinking necessary for life. Datta explains that this is due to the fact that heavy stress is put on conformity in the primary and secondary schools.[49] Comparing the educational systems in Ghana, Tanzania, and Uganda, Datta quotes Barkan, explaining:

> The educational systems of the three countries . . . have been operating within a 'hierarchical-elitist' framework, and principally by means of rote methods of instruction. Thus all the educational systems emphasized such values as industry, honesty, obedience

46. See Ethington and Wolfle, "Sex Differences."
47. Ibid., 376.
48. See Kingsbury, "Barriers and Facilitators."
49. Datta, *Education and Society.*

and craftiness, while the qualities of leadership, initiative and the critical faculty are ignored.[50]

There is great need for pedagogical methods that foster critical reflection in the life of learners in Africa, especially at the higher education level. However, given that education is cumulative, adapting transformative learning methods from primary to secondary school levels would be the best way to prepare learners in university for greater critical reflection.

CONCLUSIONS ABOUT EDUCATION IN AFRICA

The issue of lack of impact of education on the transformation of Africans and equipping them for the transformation of their communities has many root causes. First, the review of literature has demonstrated that while in other parts of the world the mother tongue is the same as the language of instruction, in Africa education was and is still conducted in foreign languages. Comprehension and critical thinking for some learners could therefore be limited by lack of adequate communication skills. On the other hand, the African learner has been detached from his mother tongue, to which colonial education did not give much attention. When the child becomes older and needs to know his or her culture, she finds it difficult to understand it because there is no such course in formal education, and if there is, there is no importance attached to it. This has contributed to the African losing part of his or her identity without becoming the colonizer whose history and culture the African learner is busy acquiring.

The second major issue that education in Africa has gone through is lack of relevance in curriculum. Even if urbanization is rapidly growing in Africa, a majority of the population lives in rural areas. Unfortunately, the curriculum in schools in Africa is tailored toward preparing people for book-related jobs rather than field work. This hinders the production of jobs in rural areas and increases the competition for the few jobs that are available in town by hundreds of graduates who migrate to towns for job hunting. In most of the cases this migration leads to the survival of the fittest, consequently young boys are able to get jobs in towns but young girls remain suffering in rural areas. This also increases the gap in the ratio of male to female employees. As a result, young girls are discouraged from

---

50. Barkan, *African Dilemma*, 37.

pursuing education because they are not encouraged by their older females who graduate from school yet remain unemployed.

Third, the literature review has clearly shown that education in Africa is suffering much from lack of funding. This is not surprising considering that many governments in Africa function because of donations from outside. Lack of funding affects the physical infrastructures of the school, the students and their teachers. In many situations poor performance is attributed to poor infrastructure and lack of support material. Also, lack of funds contributes to teachers' low salaries. This makes good teachers move away to search for "greener pastures," either in private sectors, in neighboring countries, or abroad.[51] This is the reason why many schools in Africa do not have teachers. Even some that have teachers do not have competent ones. Furthermore, teachers who remain in schools are overwhelmed with many students in their classes, especially in primary school where most of the governments are now offering free primary education.

Finally, education in Africa lacks quality. The main reason for this lack of quality is pedagogical. The colonial system which placed the teacher at the center of learning did not prepare the learner for transformation. Rote memorization and fact-giving could not prepare the learner for free reflection that could lead him or her to personal discovery, new invention, and inner reflection.

Comparing the above four critical issues, I would say that the last one is the most vital. Even if Africa received millions of dollars for education, if Africans themselves are not able to be innovative, the funding can work for some time but cannot solve the problem of Africans. It is only after Africans have been transformed and equipped to transform their society that true development will occur on the continent. Otherwise, globalization could be more devastating to Africans than before. We therefore need a new type of educational philosophy, different from the existing one which has its root in the colonial philosophy of education. We need a transformative learning which could transform and equip the sons and daughters of Africa to transform their communities. The following domain will deal with such a form of education.

51. See Manik, "To Greener Pastures."

3

Theory of Education for Holistic Transformation

INTRODUCTION

Holistic transformation is a process of becoming critically aware of one's personal, historical, cultural, social, relational and spiritual contexts which leads to changing the assumptions and frames of references, resulting in perspective transformation of meaning which in turn empowers the learner to respond to his or her life circumstances with a wider repertoire of possible actions. Becoming critically aware is the outcome of critical reflection which only comes through critical thinking. As Fetherstone and Kelly put it, "It is through reflection that we can recognize problems, as well as the ways that problems are framed, and take steps to solve them."[1] According to Mezirow, critical reflection is derived from "the unquenchable human search for meaning and coherence."[2] The review of literature for the theory of holistic transformation includes a brief description of the origin of transformative learning, the role and process of cognitive transformation, affective/relational transformation, spiritual transformation and social/community transformation.

---

1. Fetherston and Kelly, "Conflict Resolution and Transformative Pedagogy," 268.
2. Mezirow et al., *Fostering Critical Reflection*, 11.

ORIGIN AND DEVELOPMENT OF TRANSFORMATIVE LEARNING

Jack Mezirow's theory of transformative learning has been in the literature for more than thirty years now. The theory emerged from a large qualitative study (1978) of women returning to community college after an extended period of being away from formal education settings. Mezirow wanted to know the changes in roles and self-concepts that the women experienced as a result of participating in the college programs and the processes that led to those changes. Mezirow's interest was therefore in both the changes and the processes that had led to that change. The findings revealed that as the women became critically aware of their personal, historical, and cultural contexts, their assumptions and frames of references changed, resulting in perspective transformations.

Mezirow was influenced by other theories such as Kuhn's paradigm, Freire's conscientization, and Habermas's domains of learning.[3] Kuhn's (1970) conception of paradigms provided a basis for Mezirow's notion of transformative learning. During a one-year period at the Center of Advanced Studies in the Behavioral Sciences, Kuhn wrote an essay on the history and nature of science. In the process of writing the essay, he realized that there was a major disagreement between the social scientists and the natural scientists as to what constituted legitimate scientific inquiry. Investigating the source of disagreement, Kuhn theorized the importance of paradigms, which he defined as "universally recognized scientific achievements that for a time provide model problems and solutions to a community of practitioners."[4] Mezirow referred to Kuhn's paradigm to explain the frame of reference.[5] Other terms that Mezirow borrowed from Kuhn involve perspective transformation, meaning perspective and habits of mind.

Like Kuhn's (1970) paradigm, the work of Paulo Freire also informed Mezirow's (1975) initial theories. Freire called the traditional education a "banking" method of learning, whereby the teacher deposits information to those students whom the teacher deems worthy of receiving the gift of knowledge. The major problem with this form of education is that students become dependent on the teacher for knowledge and do not learn to think

---

3. See Kuhn, *Structure of Scientific Revolutions*; Freire, *Pedagogy of the Oppressed*; and Habermas, *Knowledge and Human Interests*.

4. Kuhn, *Structure of Scientific Revolutions*, 82.

5. See Mezirow, *Critical Theory of Self-Directed Learning*; *Transformative Dimensions of Adult Learning*; "Transformation Theory and Cultural Context."

for themselves. Freire points out, "The more students work at storing the deposits entrusted to them, the less they develop the critical consciousness which would result from their intervention in the world as transformers of that world."[6] Freire's antidote to this reliance on someone else and the lack of free thought was conscientization and its emphasis on developing a consciousness that has the power to transform reality. Freire defined consciousness as "learning to perceive social, political, and economic contradictions—developing a critical awareness—so that individuals can take action against the oppressive elements of reality."[7]

According to Freire, for education to be empowering the teacher needs not only to be democratic but also to form a transformative relationship between him or her and the students, students and their learning, and students and society. For Freire, education does not stop in the classroom but continues in all aspects of a learner's life. For Freire and Faundez, before the classroom can be democratic the teacher has to welcome input from the students as well as present critical ideas for discussion so that they "affirm themselves without thereby disaffirming their students."[8]

Freire distinguishes two levels of consciousness. For him, the lowest level that he calls "intransitive thought" occurs when people feel that their lives are out of their control and that change is up to fate or God. They fanatically believe that their actions cannot change their conditions and feel disempowered with little hope for the future. The next stage, "semi-transitive," involves thoughts and action for change, but an individual at this level addresses problems one at a time and as they occur rather than seeing the problem as one of society in general. The highest level of "critical transitivity" is reflected in individuals who think globally and critically about their present conditions and who decide to take action for change. These people are able to merge critical thought with critical action to effect change in their lives and to see what the catalyst for that change could be. It is this last stage of critical consciousness that clearly influenced Mezirow in his notions of disorienting dilemma, critical reflection, critical self-reflection on assumptions, and critical discourse.[9]

---

6. Freire, *Pedagogy of the Oppressed*, 60.
7. Ibid., 19.
8. Freire and Faundez, *Learning to Question*, 34.
9. Mezirow, *Education for Perspective Transformation*; "Perspective Transformation"; and *Critical Theory of Self-Directed Learning*.

Finally, Habermas also influenced Mezirow's theory of transformative learning. From 1956 to 1959 Habermas studied at the Frankfort Institute for Social Research. In 1984 he wrote a two-volume work stressing the importance of people communicating with each other in an effort to come to a common understanding so that it was not "the relation of a solitary subject to something in the objective world that can be represented or manipulated, but the inter-subjective relation that speaking and acting subjects take up when they come to an understanding with one another about something."[10] However, Habermas influenced Mezirow mainly in his critical theory of adult learning and adult education. Habermas has proposed three domains of learning: (a) the technical (learning that is rote, specific to a task, and clearly governed by rules); (b) the practical (which involves social norms, teachers who understand how to interact in an online chat room would be experiencing practical learning); and (c) the emancipatory (which is introspective as the learner is self-reflective and experiences self-knowledge).[11] Mezirow's examination of these three domains led to his description of perspective transformation as

> the emancipatory process of becoming critically aware of how and why the structure of psycho-cultural assumptions has come to constrain the way we see ourselves and our relationships, reconstituting this structure to permit a more inclusive and discriminating integration of experience and acting upon these new understandings.[12]

Based on his research with adult learners, Mezirow outlines "a theory of adult development and a derivative concept of adult education."[13] Mezirow's initial theory became more developed as he expanded the view of perspective transformation by relating the emancipator process to self-directed learning to form three revised types of learning.[14] The original three types of learning (technical, practical, and emancipator) based on Habermas's work became (a) instrumental, (b) dialogic, and (c) self-reflective.[15] Simply stated, learners ask how they could best learn the information

10. Habermas, *Knowledge and Human Interests*, 392.
11. Ibid.
12. Mezirow, "Critical Theory of Adult Learning," 6.
13. Mezirow, *Education for Perspective Transformation*, 153.
14. Ibid. See also Mezirow, "Perspective Transformation."
15. Mezirow, *Critical Theory of Self-Directed Learning*; cf. Habermas, *Knowledge and Human Interests*.

Theory of Education for Holistic Transformation

(instrumental), when and where this learning could best take place (dialogic), and why they are learning the information (self-reflection). Central to the perspective transformation and therefore, the three types of learning, are the meaning perspective and the meaning schemes.

A meaning perspective refers "to the structure of cultural and psychological assumptions within which our past experience assimilates and transforms new experience,"[16] whereas a meaning scheme is "the constellation of concept, belief, judgment, and feeling which shapes a particular interpretation."[17] Mezirow explains that within each of the three learning types, three learning processes operate: learning within meaning schemes (learners working with what they already know by expanding on, complementing, and revising their present systems of knowledge); learning new meaning schemes (that are compatible with existing schemes within the learner's meaning perspectives); and learning through meaning transformation (becoming aware of specific assumptions—schemata, criteria, rules, or repressions—on which a distorted or incomplete meaning scheme is based and, through a reorganization of meaning, transforming it).[18]

Learning through meaning transformation results in perspective transformation, which can occur in two dimensions: through an accumulation or concatenation of transformations in set meaning schemes,[19] or it can be an epochal and painful transformation of meaning perspectives, or sets of meaning schemes, as this dimension involves a comprehensive and critical re-evaluation of oneself. Mezirow argued that the central element to the perspective transformation is critical self-reflection.[20] In other words, if a learner rationalized a new point of view without dealing with the deep feelings that accompanied the original meaning scheme or perspective, perspective transformation could not occur.

In 1991, Mezirow expanded the original ten-phase model of perspective transformation to include an additional phase: "renegotiating relationships and negotiating new relationships."[21] He further outlined the constructivist assumptions that formed the basis of the revised theory as

---

16. Mezirow, *Critical Theory of Self-Directed Learning*, 21.
17. Mezirow, "Understanding Transformation Theory," 223.
18. Mezirow, *Critical Theory of Self-Directed Learning*, 23.
19. Ibid.
20. See Mezirow, *Transformative Dimensions of Adult Learning*; "Understanding Transformation Theory."
21. Mezirow, *Transformative Dimensions of Adult Learning*, 224.

including "a conviction that meaning exists within ourselves rather than in external forms such as books and that personal meanings that we attribute to our experience are acquired and validated through human interaction and communication."[22] Mezirow now contended that there are three types of meaning perspectives: epistemic (related to knowledge and how a person uses knowledge), sociolinguistic (related to language and how it is used in social settings), and psychological (related to the way people viewed themselves).[23] According to Mezirow, change takes place when the learner takes a new perspective compared to the initial distorted assumptions.[24] According to Merwe and Albertyn, these distorted assumptions could be psychological (the fear of failure and new challenges, the lack of belief in their own abilities, and feeling inhibited and inferior); sociolinguistic (limitations caused by social structures and social rules); and epistemic (the way people use knowledge).[25]

To shed light on transformative learning, Duerr, Zajonc and Dana conducted a study whose purpose was to document academic programs and other initiatives in North American universities and colleges that incorporate transformative and spiritual elements of learning.[26] The responses from the respondents indicated that transformation was used in the classrooms or in their academic programs, and ninety percent of the respondents rated contemplative and spiritual dimensions of learning as important or very important. Some respondents gave a holistic definition about transformative learning. O'Sullivan, one of the respondents and professor of transformative learning at Toronto University, Canada, defined transformative learning as follows:

> Transformative learning involves experiencing a deep, structural shift in the basic premises of thoughts, feelings, and action. It is a shift in consciousness that dramatically and permanently alters our way of being in the world. Such a shift involves our understanding of ourselves and our self-location; our relationships with other humans and with the natural world; our understanding of relations of power in interlocking structures of class, race and gender; our body-awareness, our visions of alternative approaches to

22. Ibid., xiv.
23. Ibid.
24. Ibid.
25. Van der Merwe and Albertyn, "Transformation through Training."
26. Duerr et al., "Survey of Transformative and Spiritual Dimensions."

living; and our sense of possibilities for social justice and peace and personal joy.[27]

Some other respondents noted the need for conceiving transformation beyond the individual and extended it to the community. Another respondent said: "Transformative learning is any experience that results in enhanced self-awareness, community awareness, and further participation in efforts that serve individual and community growth."

Respondents indicated that the process of transformative learning in the classroom is supported or facilitated by certain pedagogical practices such as collaborative learning (over 90% of respondents), experiential pedagogy such as participatory learning and experiences in other cultures (over 90%), contemplative practices (86.7%), autobiographical techniques (86.7%), service learning (76.7%) and creative or artistic expressions (73.3%).

Speaking about strategies in the future that could contribute to transformative learning with cognitive and spiritual dimensions together, the respondents suggested the need for research, funding, support for such activities, educating administrators, dialoguing with others with the same interest, and building a strategy for the future of transformative learning.[28]

In any discussion of transformative learning, the context is very important and one would ask, what is the role of context in transformative learning? How does culture and socio-economic background affect transformative learning? To answer such questions, Merriam and Ntseane conducted a study to examine how culture shapes the process of transformative learning.[29] The study is built on the assumption that transformative learning in Africa should be conceived as an individual experience but one that is contextualized in the individuals' interpretation and meaning-making of the environment and culture.

The study was guided by the question "How did the cultural context of Botswana shape the way participants processed and interpreted the event?" The study found that the disorienting dilemma that precipitates the process consisted of life events such as death of a child, illness, car accident, betrayal, etc. Three culturally specific factors shaped the cultural contexts of the transformative process: spirituality and the metaphysical world, community responsibilities and relationships, and gender roles.

27. Ibid., 185.
28. Ibid., 192–98.
29. See Merriam and Ntseane, "Transformational Learning in Botswana."

This study is an example of African worldview which is holistic. The African mind is not dichotomized; rather, it operates as a whole, with the spiritual taking the core part of life. As Léopold Sédar Senghor puts it, "The Negro African does not just see something; he feels it."[30] This psychological intuition can be both dangerous and useful. It can be dangerous if used without a sense of reflection and critical thinking. But it can be useful because it serves as a gate to the spiritual and moral developments.

The second issue that the study reveals is the importance of community for an African person. He is because he belongs. This principle can also be useful if used with the idea that individuals form a community. But if it is conceived in the sense that a community forms individuals, then community becomes more important than individuals and individuals lose their freedom. Another danger for this would be for individuals to make a wrong decision even when they know in their conscience that it is wrong but because it is upheld by the community values and ideology they nevertheless do it!

CRITICAL REFLECTION IN TRANSFORMATIVE LEARNING

Generally speaking, transformation does not come from a good learning experience, but from an effective reflection of that learning experience. That is why Mezirow and other transformational educators have continued to emphasize the importance of critical reflection in transformative learning theory. Mezirow calls "straightforward reflection" the act of "intentional assessment" of one's actions,[31] whereas "critical reflection" not only involves the nature and consequence of one's actions but also includes the related circumstances of their origin.

Merriam argues that being able to critically reflect, and in particular to critically self-reflect on our own assumptions as well as those of others, which involves critique of a premise upon which the learner has defined a problem, mandates an advanced level of cognitive development.[32] This is because, as she further explains, to be able to engage in reflective discourse with others assumes the ability to examine alternative perspectives,

---

30. Dubois and Wijngaert, *Initiation philosophique*, 334.
31. Mezirow, *Critical Theory of Self-Directed Learning*, 144.
32. Merriam, "Role of Cognitive Development," 61.

Theory of Education for Holistic Transformation

withhold premature judgment, and basically to think dialectically, a characteristic of mature cognitive development.[33]

Types of Reflection

Mezirow presented three types of reflection and their roles in transforming meaning schemes and perspectives: content reflection, process reflection, and premise reflection.[34] Content reflection involves thinking back to what was done and, therefore, might involve a transformation of a meaning scheme. It is thinking about the actual experience itself. Process reflection is thinking about how to handle the experience. Finally, premise reflection requires the person to see the larger view of what is operating within his or her value system, for instance, and could transform a meaning perspective rather than a meaning scheme. It is examining long-held, socially constructed assumptions, beliefs, and values about the experience or problem. In summary of the three types of reflection, learners can transform an individual meaning scheme by examining previous actions (content reflection of learning within meaning scheme), or where the actions and their related factors originated (process reflection or learning new meaning schemes), but when they consider a more global view, the reflection is much deeper, more complex, and involves transforming a series of meaning schemes (premise reflection or learning through meaning transformation).

According to Mezirow, reflection is important at two points. First, after experiencing a disorienting dilemma that sets the process in motion, the learner engages in self-examination that is often accompanied by feelings of fear, anger, guilt or shame.[35] Second, reflection is important at the step of a critical assessment of assumptions, or premise reflection.

Aspects of Critical Reflection

In his work (1998a), Mezirow presented two new aspects of critical reflection: critical reflection of assumptions, where the learner not only looks back on something that occurred but also examines the assumptions or presuppositions that were involved in the reflection process (content and

---

33. Ibid.
34. Mezirow, *Transformative Dimensions of Adult Learning*.
35. Mezirow et al., *Learning as Transformation*, 22.

process reflection). The other new aspect was the related concept of critical self-reflection of assumption, which involves a critique of a premise upon which the learner has defined the problem. In this way, critical self-reflection of an assumption is akin to premise reflection. Learners examine their worldview in light of their own particular belief or value system.

Taxonomy of Critical Reflection

Mezirow (1998b) articulated a taxonomy of critical reflection of and on assumptions that involved objective reframing and subjective reframing. Subjective reframing is a consideration of the assumption, whereas objective reframing is a consideration on what caused the assumption to occur. Objective reframing is either a narrative critical reflection of assumptions and requires critically examining something that was being communicated to a person, or an action critical reflection of assumptions. In this case it requires taking a moment to critically consider one's own assumptions in a task-oriented problem-solving situation to define the problem itself (e.g., considering what you believe would constitute the worth of an educational technology project).

Subjective reframing is more of a critical self-reflection rather than critical assumptions. It can include one of four forms of critical self-reflection on assumptions:

(a) Narrative critical self-reflection on assumptions: the application of narrative critical reflection of assumptions to oneself (considering the problem as applied to self and coming to a resolution);

(b) Systematic critical self-reflection on assumptions: going beyond the action critical reflection of assumptions to self-reflect on the taken-for-granted cultural influences, which might be organizational or moral ethical;

(c) Therapeutic critical self-reflection on assumptions: examining one's problematic feelings and their related consequences;

(d) Epistemic critical self-reflection on assumptions: investigating not only the assumptions but also the causes, the nature, and the consequences of one's frame of reference to surmise why one is predisposed to learn in a certain manner.

Mezirow's taxonomy of learning is not very far from Bloom's taxonomy in the cognitive domain. According to Yount, Bloom formulated six levels

Theory of Education for Holistic Transformation

in the cognitive domain: knowledge, comprehension, application, analysis, synthesis, and evaluation.[36] Knowledge is recalling the past. Comprehension is obtaining meaning from communication or processing information. Application is using the information in a novel situation. Analysis is the first of the three higher levels of cognitive domain, and means breaking something down into its parts. Synthesis, which is the second highest level of cognition, is creating something new by combining different ideas. Finally, evaluation is judging the value of material according to specific criteria.

Ways of Learning

Mezirow refined his previous theory of ways of learning and added a fourth one.[37] The first is elaborating on existing frames of reference (or meaning perspective). The second is learning new frames of reference. The third is transforming habits of mind. The fourth is transforming points of view. Regarding the process of learning, Mezirow et al. noted that transformative learning often involves two processes, an "objective re-framing" whereby we begin to understand the wider issue of power, socialization, and the history involved in how we come to be, and a "subjective re-framing" that involves the personal difficulties of working through and confronting change.[38]

To illustrate the pedagogical methods used in transformative learning, a study was conducted by Fetherstone and Kelly between January and June 2006 to track the impact on students of a fundamental revision of a first-year course, *Introduction to Conflict Resolution*.[39] The purpose of the study was to understand the students' experiences of learning within the revised methodology and the possibilities of transformative learning through the course.

The research was guided by five transformative learning presuppositions about transformative education and critical pedagogy, which are:

(1) Transformative learning involves profound shifts in our understanding of knowledge, the world, and ourselves;

(2) Reflection is key to the achievement of transformation;

---

36. Yount, *Created to Learn*.
37. See Mezirow et al., *Learning as Transformation*.
38. Ibid., 22–23.
39. See Fetherstone and Kelly, "Conflict Resolution and Transformative Pedagogy."

(3) Transformation is a process precipitated by experiences or information that disrupt current understanding;

(4) Teaching for transformation involves creating spaces for critical engagement and dialogue; and

(5) The concept of transformative learning resonates with an education for conflict transformation.

The finding revealed four distinctive clusters of experience of the Conflict Resolution pedagogy. The first cluster was the "not getting it." These were the learners who revealed a limited understanding of the pedagogy and reflection, as well as an unwillingness to engage in a process of critical examination of their beliefs. They would be angry or accusatory, sanitized or strategic, or disengaged with a denial attitude.[40] The second cluster was that of transitional/challenges. This was a cluster whereby students began to come to grips with the course material and methodology. They began to articulate for themselves where they fit into the course, how they wanted or could engage with it, and enunciated the challenges and blocks to doing that successfully.[41] Third, the "getting it" / challenge was the next stage leading to employing with more deliberation and reflection the new information, understanding, awareness and skills gained in the course and methodology. Finally, the transitional/disruptions was the stage whereby students had clearly moved beyond change but had not achieved transformation.

In their analysis, the researchers explained the resistance from students' learning from low motivation, apathy, and disinterest with respect to the new pedagogy. "Students expected and wanted knowledge 'delivered' by an 'expert,' which they could bank and later reproduce in an essay/exam."[42]

Discussing factors that facilitate change, the researchers point out familiarity with the process and with people, and understanding that developed through the semester, the development of skills learning, the base groups (peer relationships), positive interdependence (promotive interaction), learning and development through empowerment (promotion of use of reflective diaries to think about the learning process, the class environment, and group dynamics).

Explaining why students did not reach true transformation, the researchers suggest that the plateau of change may have occurred because

---

40. Ibid., 272.
41. Ibid., 273.
42. Ibid., 274.

Theory of Education for Holistic Transformation

the course was taught as an academic discipline, not considering so much the role of emotions in learning. The researchers refer to Boyd and Myers, who explain that "transformative learning is not only or even a 'rational-ordered' set of processes but also, significantly, engages non-rational meaning making involving emotion, intuition, disordering and mess."[43] The most important contribution of this study is that not all experiences lead to true transformation, and that emotions play a key role in the transformative process.

Another study conducted by Freeman, Alston, and Winborne at Howard University and Talladega examined if students' attitudes, motivation, and learning were enhanced as a result of participating in linked courses (two courses on which faculty collaborate) and the clustered ones (more than two courses on which faculty collaborate).[44] Specifically, the research was guided by the following questions:

- What is the nature and level of a student's motivation in STEM (Science, Technology, Engineering and Mathematics) classes?
- Is motivation enhanced as a result of the learning community initiative?
- Do students report positive or negative attitudes about linked STEM courses?

The authors concluded that learning communities seem especially fitting for African American students, and suggest that they can be considered culturally relevant pedagogy for African American students throughout the education pipeline. This study is based on an important educational theory of collaborative pedagogy of learning communities which explains how a learning community can increase motivation, thus leading to higher learning productivity.

Relating the finding to the study of transformative learning, both findings during the pre- and post-test corroborate the need of trusting relationships in transformative learning. The study shows that at the pre-test, intrinsic motivation was lowest among the students and extrinsic motivation highest. Yet at post-test self-efficacy beliefs were strongly and positively related to intrinsic motivation, task value, and control of learning beliefs. During the pre-test students had not yet developed trust, but at the

---

43. Boyd and Myers, "Transformative Education," 277.
44. Freeman et al., "Do Learning Communities."

post-test period trust was already built, therefore increasing the intrinsic motivation.

Speaking about pedagogical methods fostering transformative learning, another study was conducted by Adkins-Coleman to document the beliefs and practices of teachers who successfully facilitated engagement among black students.[45] The analysis of the finding resulted in the following five themes.

Facilitating Motivation

The two teachers articulated the belief of some scholars such as Ladson-Billings, who posit that successful teachers of black students are the ones highly involved in the social and emotional development of their students.[46] For example, Ms. Lomax had this to say about her students:

> Their acceptance of learning is connected with whether or not they think you like them. Black kids, I think, are more open to learning different things, but they're not willing to learn from people who they feel don't have their best interest at heart. Black kids are more "show me you care about me before I ask you for what you know," and I think that's the greatest difference [between teaching black students and white students].[47]

Strong Relationships and Mutual Respect

Both teachers in this study understood the importance of relationships and believed it was important for students to see their teacher's commitment to them in words and actions. Ms. Morrison said this:

> Another teacher's worst student is a good student for me, so I don't have any I would be glad to get rid of . . . When they step in the room, they're mine and it's like a child. You just can't get rid of your child if they've done something wrong . . .[48]

---

45. Adkins-Coleman, "I Am Not Afraid."
46. Ibid., 45.
47. Ibid., 45.
48. Ibid., 46.

Building Empathy through Words and Actions

Both teachers in this study showed great care and empathy when students shared their feelings about personal and academic issues. They both seemed to understand the importance of verbal and nonverbal communication.

Maintaining High Behavioral Expectation

Researchers have found that black students generally show respect for teachers who speak and act with authority.[49] This is because, as Irvine noted, these teachers understand the urgency for black students to learn in order to ensure future opportunities, so they insist on it.[50] These teachers are called "warm demanders," and Ms. Morrison expressed beliefs that are consistent with the characteristics of warm demanders. For instance, Ms. Morrison said:

> This is my classroom and you're going to respect my classroom and there is no compromising in that. This is mine and there are the rules and that's it, and you just stick to that and you don't have a problem and [the students] understand it.[51]

Engaging Students in Cognitive Tasks

In Ms. Morrison's classroom, students remained engaged because there was no alternative. She expected them to learn, she treated them as if they were capable of learning, and she truly believed they wanted to learn. Ms. Lomax required her students to examine literature at par with upper-level college English courses, but she provided an unlimited amount of support to ensure students' success. In addition to the above pedagogical practices, the two teachers created engaging academically rigorous communities from the beginning of the school year.

---

49. Bondy et al., "Creating Environments of Success"; Brown, "We Were All Slaves"; Delpit, *Other People's Children's Cultural Conflicts*.
50. Irvine, "Education of Children," cited by Adkins-Coleman, "I'm Not Afraid."
51. Adkins-Coleman, "I'm Not Afraid," 47.

AFFECTIVE/RELATIONAL DIMENSION OF TRANSFORMATIVE LEARNING

We have seen the cognitive domain which deals with knowledge and concept development. The affective domain emphasizes attitudes and values. According to Yount, Bloom's taxonomy summarizes the development of the affective domain into five levels: receiving or willingness to listen or attending to something; responding or participating actively by expressing one's opinion; valuing or expressing a belief or attitude about the value or worth of something; organizing or integrating new values into one's general set of values; and characterizing or acting consistently with a new value.[52]

Taylor points out that the idea of transformative learning has moved beyond Mezirow's dominant conception to include attention to the emotional and affective dimensions of transformation and recognition of the centrality of relationships in the transformative learning process.[53] What Mezirow calls "perspective transformation" is nothing less than a paradigm shift. A perspective transformation leads to a more fully developed (more functional) frame of reference—one that is inclusive, differentiating, permeable, critically reflective, and an integrative experience. According to Mezirow, a perspective transformation often occurs either through a series of cumulative transformed meaning schemes or as a result of an acute personal or social crisis such as a natural disaster, the death of a significant other, divorce, war, job loss, or retirement.[54] These experiences are often stressful and painful, and they can cause individuals to question the very core of their existence.

As seen earlier, the process of transformative learning begins with a disorientation of some kind, variously described as disruption of one's worldview, frame of reference, meaning perspective, or taken-for-granted assumptions. In Mezirow's formula, the process begins with a disorienting dilemma which leads to a self-examination with others (in mutual dialogue), a critical assessment of internalized assumptions, and finally a perspective transformation or a new meaning perspective. Such frames of reference are better than others because they are more likely to generate beliefs and opinions that will prove true or justified to guide to action.[55]

---

52. Yount, *Created to Learn*.
53. Taylor, "Update on Transformative Learning Theory."
54. Mezirow, "Perspective Transformation."
55. Mezirow, "Transformative Learning as Discourse," 58–59.

So, what are the triggers for such a disorienting dilemma? Brookfield suggests that an educator may set out to disrupt comfortable worldviews held by participants as in the practice of ideology critique, but other writers suggest that in other instances the disorienting is generated by an external event, such as a personal illness, the loss of a job, a cultural dislocation.[56] For Cranton, fostering transformative learning in the classroom depends to a large extent on establishing meaningful, genuine relationships with students.[57] Relationships begin with the sense of authenticity. Jarvis suggests that people are being authentic when they choose to act so as to "foster the growth and development of each other's being."[58] Jarvis states that teachers and students learn together through dialogue; the result of authentic teaching is that "teachers learn and grow together with their students."[59]

Cranton notes that "as the frame of reference for the concept of 'student' becomes more open and permeable through transformative learning, students and educators can develop genuine relationships in which the educator makes a difference in the students' lives and feels a difference in his or her own life as well."[60] To enter into an authentic relationship with students, teachers need to have a good understanding of themselves. Cranton calls this self-awareness.[61] In addition to self-awareness, teachers need to understand others. Speaking about relationships, Cranton describes three kinds of teacher-student relationships. Educators may form relationships based on respectful distance, collegiality, or closeness.

Brookfield proposed that being an authentic teacher includes making sure our behaviors are congruent with our words, admitting we do not have all the answers and can make mistakes, building trust with students through revealing personal aspects of ourselves and our experiences, and respecting students as people.[62] Jarvis states: "When people's actions are controlled by others and their performance is repetitive and ritualistic, we have in-authenticity . . . We are authentic when we choose to act so as to foster the growth and development of each other's being."[63] Buber affirms

56. Brookfield, "Transformative Learning as Ideology Critique."
57. Cranton, *Understanding and Promoting Transformative Learning*.
58. Jarvis, *Paradoxes of Learning*, 113.
59. Ibid., 114.
60. Cranton, *Understanding and Promoting Transformative Learning*, 8.
61. Ibid.
62. Brookfield, *Skillful Teacher*.
63. Jarvis, *Paradoxes of Learning*, 113–14.

that it is only through relationships with others that authenticity can be fostered.[64] Heidegger invokes critical participation and explains:

> We question how we are different from the community and live accordingly; we do not do something just because it is done that way by others or believe without considering whether it is true for us. This is a good way of understanding authenticity—we need to know who we are and what we believe and then act on that.[65]

Hollis helped us to integrate our understanding of persona with the importance of relationships in authenticity. According to Hollis, to enter into an authentic relationship requires self-understanding. He points out, "The quality of all our relationships is a direct function of our relationship to ourselves . . . The best thing we can do for our relationships with others, and with the transcendent, then, is to render our relationship to ourselves more conscious."[66] Cranton and Roy conclude that authenticity is the expression of the genuine self in the community, and that to create that genuine self, we need to critically participate in life rather than run with the unconscious herd. Part of this journey is understanding how others are different from us without attempting to make them into our own image; that is, we help others discover their authenticity as a way of fostering our own authenticity.[67] Cranton and Roy conclude that "every transformative experience leads to further authenticity."[68]

As seen earlier in other literature review, trust is at the center of the dynamics of relationships between the facilitator and the learner. In regard to this, a study was conducted by Webber to examine the development of two dimensions of trust in student project teams over the course of a semester.[69] The study was based on the following hypotheses:

(1) Early trust will be one-dimensional;

(2) Trust measured at the end of the team's life span, "established" trust, will be two-dimensional, and cognitive and affective trust will be related but distinct components;

(3) Familiarity with team members will be positively related to early trust;

64. Buber, *I and Thou*.
65. Heidegger, *Being and Time*, 10.
66. Hollis, *Eden Project*, 13.
67. Cranton and Roy, "When the Bottom Falls Out," 94.
68. Ibid.
69. Webber, "Development of Cognitive and Affective Trust."

Theory of Education for Holistic Transformation

(4a) Interaction frequency will be positively and significantly related to affective trust after controlling familiarity, and early trust and interaction frequency will not be positively and significantly related to cognitive trust; (4b) Citizenship behaviors will be positively and significantly related to cognitive trust;

(5) Reliable performance will be positively and significantly related to cognitive trust after controlling for familiarity and early trust, and reliable performance will not be positively and significantly related to affective trust;

(6) Monitoring behaviors will be negatively and significantly related to cognitive and affective trust after controlling for familiarity and early trust;

(7a) The relationship between reliable performance and cognitive trust is moderated by early trust such that reliable performance will be more strongly related to cognitive trust when early trust is high; (7b) The relationship between interaction frequency and affective trust will be moderated by early trust such that interaction frequency and affective trust when early trust such interaction frequency will be more strongly related to affective trust when early trust is high; (7c) The relationship between citizenship behaviors and affective trust will be moderated by early trust such that citizenship behaviors will be more strongly related to affective trust when early trust is high;

(8) Cognitive and affective trust will have a positive significant relationship with team performance; however, the relationship with affective trust will be stronger.

The findings from this study is summarized into four propositions:

(1) Early trust emerges as a one-dimensional factor early in the life span of the team;

(2) Cognitive and affective trust emerge as separate components over time;

(3) Unique and distinct predictors affect early trust, cognitive trust, and affective trust; and

(4) Cognitive and affective trust do differentially affect team performance.

Relating the finding to the study of transformation, this study supports the importance of trust and its relationship to the affective rather than cognitive life as seen earlier. The finding of hypothesis 8, that "cognitive trust was not significantly related to team performance and affective trust was significantly and positively related to team performance," is very important in our discussion about transformation.

Another study was conducted by Wighting and Jing.[70] The purpose of the study was to measure and examine relationships between school community and religious commitment among high school students, and to respond to the following research questions:

(1) Is there a relationship between sense of community and religious commitment?

(2) Are there any significant differences between boys and girls in either sense of community or religious commitment?

The results indicated that there was a moderate correlation between sense of community and religious commitment. It seemed that the correlation was higher for females than for males. Also, there was significant relationship between learning community and intrapersonal religious commitment and between learning community and interpersonal religious commitment. Finally, a significant relationship existed between social and intrapersonal religious commitment.

The researchers explained the correlation between sense of religious commitment and sense of community by the fact that students attending Christian schools have grown up in Christian homes where they view Christian commitment and Christian community as being at least interdependent. The researchers paid attention to the gender difference in the finding, and encouraged teachers in Christian schools to organize projects that require interaction between boys and girls. This would help boys to be motivated by girls' commitment. Also, the researchers encouraged administrators in Christian high schools to indirectly increase students' learning by taking active measures to promote a sense of whole-school community.

In relation to transformative learning, this study confirms that learning in community can be more transformative than individual learning alone. Social commitment has an effect on intra-personal commitment due to the role that motivation, modeling and mutual encouragement play in group dynamics.

In the same vein, Zhao and Kuh conducted a study whose purpose was to discover whether participation in a learning community was linked with

70. Wighting and Jing, "Relationships."

Theory of Education for Holistic Transformation

students' success, broadly defined as student engagement in educationally purposeful activities, self-reported gains in a variety of desired outcomes of college, and overall satisfaction with their college experience.[71] The study was guided by five questions:

1. What is the relationship between participating in a learning community and students' academic performance?
2. What is the relationship between participating in a learning community and student engagement in a range of educationally productive activities (academic effort, academic integration, active and collaborative learning, integration with faculty members, diversity-related activities, and the extent to which classes emphasize higher order thinking)?
3. What is the relationship between participating in a learning community and students' perceptions of the degree to which their campus supports their academic and social needs, the quality of academic advising, and satisfaction with their college experience?
4. What is the relationship between participating in a learning community and students' self-reported gains in personal and social development, practical competence, and general education?
5. What types of students are more and less likely to participate in a learning community?

Regarding academic performance, the study showed that students who participated in learning communities had lower entering scores than their counterparts who did not participate. It was found out that participating in a learning community might have a salutary effect on academic performance.

In relation to Student Engagement and Perception of Campus Environment, the results revealed that for both first-year and senior students, experience with a learning community was associated with higher levels of academic effort, academic integration and active and collaborative learning. Concerning learning outcomes, the result indicated substantial effect sizes for first-year students and for senior students.

The researchers suggested that every campus should take stock of how many and what kinds of learning communities are operating and the numbers of different groups of students who are participating in them. They

71. Zhao and Kuh, "Adding Value."

also suggested that efforts should be targeted to creating additional learning communities and attracting students to them, and that some forms of learning communities may be more educationally effective than others.

Relating the findings to the study of transformative learning, it is evident that this study reinforces the finding that active and collaborative learning methods promote transformation better than the traditional individual methods. The uniqueness in this study is that collaborative learning is especially needed for first-year students in university or college. Associating with others helps the new students to discover strategies that are needed to cope with the new academic demands. The problem, however, is how to use community learning for personal transformation without encouraging "a warm-up" attitude for some students. This is an issue especially among black students who are very much community oriented. A balance, therefore, needs to be struck in the use of community learning methods so that these communities are formed by individuals who are being transformed.

Speaking about transformation through community, Selzer conducted a study to determine the effectiveness of a seminary's training and mentoring program as it is related to job satisfaction of its graduates.[72] The research was guided by the following questions:

(1) Does the training offer job satisfaction?

(2) Were the character contracts of the Training Mentoring programs (TM) helpful in their training?

(3) Were the Competency Contracts of the TM programs helpful?

(4) Was the Mentoring Relationship of the TM Program helpful?

(5) Was the Small Group experience of the TM Program helpful?

The finding revealed that most of the respondents were either satisfied (35%) or very satisfied (56%) in their current ministerial job. Second, the Character Contracts of the TM Program were helpful for 74% of all of the respondents. It was not helpful for those who felt compelled. Character contracts were contracts listing a plan for activities to promote growth in a chosen area of character. Third, the Competency Contracts of the TM Program were helpful for 57% of all the questionnaire respondents. Competency contracts were contracts listing a plan for activities (related to the knowing, informational process, the being/reflective process, and the doing/experiential process of learning) to promote growth in a chosen area

---

72. Selzer, "Effectiveness of a Seminary's Training."

of a specific ministerial competency. Fourth, the Mentoring Relationship of the TM Program was helpful for 81% of the participants. The primary reason they cited for the appreciation of the program was the appreciation of a learned role model, being known in relationship, receiving support and encouragement, getting feedback, and experiencing authenticity, trust, and accountability. Fifth, the Small Groups experience of the TM Programs was helpful for 57% of the questionnaire participants. They said that small groups were helpful because of the value of the relationships and feeling of community, the appreciation of the encouragement and support provided by the group, the enjoyment of being with others who shared similar struggles, the feeling of safety and trust and the value of experiencing other perspectives in a group setting. Sixth, the study revealed that the mentoring relationship, a required aspect of the TM Program at Denver Seminary, was the aspect most related to current job satisfaction (57%). Also, there was a significant correlation between the number of participants who thought the mentoring aspects of the TM Program were helpful and the number of participants who continue to participate in a mentoring relationship at the present time.

The study seems to indicate that mentoring promoted growth in the program participants. The fact that a number of respondents reported that they continued on with their mentoring relationships after graduating, or that they currently utilize mentoring in their ministry practice, speaks much about graduates' perceptions of the worth of a mentoring relationship.

The findings from this study are important to explain the dynamics of transformation in community learning. Role model, support and encouragement, feedback, accountability, sense of belonging, are all concepts that depict the importance of relationships. Most of these concepts, if not all, are from the affective rather than cognitive domain. This confirms the finding of Kotter that "people change what they do less because they are given an analysis that shifts their thinking than because they are shown a truth that influences their feelings."[73] This is the reason why trust is very important in relationship. Although trust may have some cognitive elements as we will see in the coming pages, trust as an intrinsic value is more at the level of the heart than of the head. For example, a protégé will trust the mentor not so much because the mentor has knowledge but because of the way the mentor treats the protégé. When the mentor loves his protégé and cares for him or her, a trusting relationship is established between the two, and

73. Kotter, *Heart of Change*, 1.

this trust influences the protégé to disclose himself more to the mentor. This disclosure helps the mentor to know the areas in the life of the protégé that need more transformation and the time for the protégé to go through paradigm shift. Mentoring becomes, therefore, a powerful transformative method because it touches a very sensitive part of man, the heart. The heart can be won and shaped, or it can be hurt and hardened. Positively, good methods should aim at winning the heart for a purpose and shaping and sharpening it for new perspectives.

Still on the role of relationships, Martin and Trueax examined the perceptions of mentoring by early childhood teachers providing evidence for the concept of transformation for both mentor and protégé in their personal and professional development.[74] The broader research question was, "What does a mentoring experience mean to a mentor and protégé in a mentoring relationship?" They also asked the sub-question, "In the perceptions of early childhood mentors and protégés, what processes occur within the concept of a mentoring relationship that change or transform the personal and professional development of the mentor and the protégé?"

The study found out that for the protégés in the relationship, mentoring offers them a voice, a place to tell their stories and to be validated in their experience. Protégés experienced perceived differences between mentoring and student teaching in terms of the regularity of their meetings and the fact that there was a mutual, reciprocal relationship in which each participant was learning from the other. Most importantly, protégés had a voice in getting what they needed from their relationship.

SPIRITUAL DIMENSION OF TRANSFORMATIVE LEARNING

Tolliver and Tisdell recognized that Mezirow and associates tried to discuss transformative learning in a broader way, but they did not explicitly discuss the role of spirituality in transformative learning.[75] The authors believe that transformative learning is more likely to be transformative if it permeates one's self, which has a spiritual element, rather than being confined to the rational realm of critically reflecting on assumptions. The authors thus suggest that transformative learning is best facilitated through engag-

---

74. Martin and Trueax, *Transformative Dimensions of Mentoring*.

75. See Tolliver and Tisdell, "Engaging Spirituality"; cf. Mezirow et al., *Learning as Transformation*.

ing multiple dimensions of being, including the rational, affective, spiritual, imaginative, somatic, and socio-cultural domains through relevant contents and experiences.

The authors define spirituality as a connection to what is referred to as Life Force, God, a higher power or purpose, Great Spirit, or Buddha nature. It is about meaning making and a sense of wholeness, healing, and the interconnectedness of all things. According to the authors, spirituality is different from religion: it is about an individual's journey toward wholeness, whereas religions are organized communities of faith that often provide meaningful community rituals that serve as a gateway to the sacred. Spirituality is also about developing a more authentic identity. Those who value spirituality believe that there is a divine spark in each person that is central to his or her core essence or authentic self. Those who value spirituality also believe that it is possible for learners to come to a greater understanding of their core essence through transformative learning experiences that help them reclaim their authenticity. The authors agree with Cranton that authenticity is core to what spirituality is about.[76]

The authors also point out another important dimension often ignored in spirituality, that of its connection to culture. According to Fowler, spirituality is partly related to how people construct knowledge through symbolic processes and unconscious structuring processes manifested through image, symbol, and music.[77]

Tolliver and Tisdell remark that spirituality does not mean proselytizing lectures, or the imposition of a dogmatic agenda; it rather means authenticity, openness, acceptance, and honoring of the various dimensions of how people learn and construct knowledge by incorporating activities that include attention to the affective, somatic, imaginative, symbolic, cultural, and communal, as well as the rational.[78]

Sheldrake defines spirituality in a Christian perspective as "a conscious relationship with God, in Jesus Christ, through the indwelling of the Holy Spirit and in the context of the community of believers."[79]

---

76. See Cranton, *Understanding and Promoting Transformative Learning*.
77. Fowler, *Stages of Faith*, 103.
78. Tolliver and Tisdell, "Engaging Spirituality."
79. Sheldrake, "What Is Spirituality?," 8.

Spiritual Transformation through Life-Crisis Triggers

In a theoretical article, Balk explains how bereavement is a life crisis that challenges one's assumptions about human existence and provides the ground for spiritual change. Balk builds his argument on the thesis that bereavement is a crisis and crises trigger spiritual change, but only those crises that allow time reflection, whose aftermath is forever colored by the experience of the crisis, and which create a psychological imbalance or disequilibrium that resists readily being stabilized.[80]

Explaining how bereavement is a life crisis, Balk says that bereavement disrupts physical functioning, manifesting such reactions as chills, diarrhea, fatigue, and profuse sweating. Emotional manifestations include intense and long-lasting reactions such as fear, anger, and sorrow. It impacts social relationships as outsiders to the grief become noticeably uncomfortable when around the grieved. And bereavement affects spirituality by challenging the griever's very assumptions about the meaning of human essence.

Balk spends more time in the article explaining how spiritual change takes place in the bereaved life.[81] He says that spiritual change is an unfolding consciousness about the meaning of human existence, and life crisis influences this unfolding by stimulating questions about the meaning of existence. Such stimulation can produce what Fowler and Bray have called "a transformed faith consciousness."[82]

In the same vein, Bray wrote an article to explain that spiritual domains of experience may be influential to an individual's growth in the aftermath of stressful life events.[83] The purpose of the paper was to explore the role that spiritual experience might play in the process of posttraumatic growth by examining two quite different approaches to transformational growth: Lawrence Calhoun and Richard Tedeschi's post traumatic growth model,[84] and Stanislav and Christina Grof's framework of psycho-spiritual transformation.[85] The paper proposes that transpersonal psychology's explanation

---

80. Balk, "Bereavement and Spiritual Change," 486.
81. Ibid.
82. Fowler, *Stages of Faith*, 487; see also Bray, "Broader Framework."
83. Ibid.
84. Calhoun and Tedeschi, "Correlation Test."
85. Grof and Grof, *Stormy Search for Self*.

of psycho-spiritual transformation provides a useful lens through which to view posttraumatic growth.

It is established that each position accepts that stressful life events can force processes of personal reconstruction, reevaluation and learning that results in the experience of positive psychological change. Also, that from the processes new material and insights impact upon the individual's philosophy of life challenging or nullifying pre-existing schemas, and that through cognitive processing and meaning-making a new construct of the life narrative and wider worldview are established.[86] In the wake of stressful events, the individual is confronted with powerful forces of change, and the life, as it was, becomes difficult to maintain. In the struggle to reconcile themselves to the reality of shattered assumptive worlds, individuals engage in meaning-making activities that might include having to negotiate difficult existential and spiritual questions that permit the construction of a new and coherent life narrative. It is suggested that at the fundamental level of the psyche, individuals are challenged to rebalance themselves in order to relieve intense psychic and physical pain by the integration of this new knowledge and the incorporation of new behaviors, beliefs, and goals.[87]

Grof and Grof's conceptualization of crises as either a danger or opportunity for transformation[88] is echoed in Calhoun and Tedeschi's comment that for some the struggle may lead to a "much less satisfactory place" while for others it represents "much more than spiritual recovery" experienced as a deeper and more satisfying understanding of place and purpose in the world.[89] It is also generally accepted by both approaches that a positive outcome often relies upon the individual's experiential style, a positive context for the experience, an understanding and acceptance of the process and the availability of informed and consistent social support. This support should be genuine and congruent, non-judgmental and accepting, well-informed and confident about the terrain and empathic in its facilitation.[90]

It is significant that a strong support network comprising family, friends and helping professionals who are able to define the experience as natural, positive, potentially healing, healthy or initiatory is considered one of the three protective factors for spiritual emergence not becoming

---

86. Ibid., 301.
87. Ibid., 303.
88. Grof and Grof, *Spiritual Emergency*.
89. Calhoun and Tedeschi, *Handbook of Posttraumatic Growth*, 35.
90. Grof and Grof, *Spiritual Emergency*.

spiritual emergency. Ideally, in this case, family, significant friends and helping professionals are regarded as equal partners in their support, and their open attitudes to spiritual emergence and their understanding of the effects on the individual are important factors in healing. Grof and Grof agree that the outcome of growth from highly painful experiences, although not expected or sought after, can often be a "more expanded way of being."[91] Similarly, Tedeschi suggests that "wisdom, a form of learning, is achieved which leads to an enhanced ability to utilize dialectical thinking in understanding life's vicissitudes."[92] This represents for both models a level of growth that is "not simply a return to baseline; it is an experience of improvement that for some persons is deeply profound."[93]

As seen in the above two articles, pain and problems in our life can contribute, more than any other transformative learning method, to foster a greater understanding of one's core essence and can affect one's assumptions about self, others, and God. It is one of the powerful methods to make individuals discover who they are in the eyes of the Creator. This search leads to true authenticity. But the process is not easy as is seen above; it can be bitter and sour. That is why the person going through such a journey needs support from relatives, close friends, or professionals who are loving, trustworthy, accepting, and caring.

In support of the spiritual dimension of transformative learning, Murshida and Kalyani conducted a study in Singapore which examined different coping mechanisms engaged by Malay/Muslim bereaved youths following parental death.[94] Positing that the spiritual dimension of death requires that helping professionals understand how spirituality can be harnessed as a resource in the healing process, the study was made of a sample of 16 Malay/Muslim youths from the ages of 12 to 23.

The finding classified the coping strategies in three categories: spirituality-focused coping, problem-solving coping, and emotion-focused coping. Spirituality was found to be used not only as a coping tool but also as a framework for the youths to understand and cope with the loss of their parents and the attendant challenges. The study revealed that the bereaved had increased reflections on death and its relationship with the

---

91. Grof and Grof, *Stormy Search*, 34.
92. Tedeschi et al., *Posttraumatic Growth*, 233.
93. Calhoun and Tedeschi, "Foundations of Posttraumatic Growth," 101.
94. See Murshidah and Kalyani, "Grief Experience."

Theory of Education for Holistic Transformation

transcendent.[95] The more the youth pondered on issues related to death, the closer they felt they were to Allah. Most of them shared that they consciously increased their efforts to learn more about Islam. The youth shared that the death actually changed their perceptions about life itself. Here is one such testimony:

> Last time I would get very angry very easily. I had a bad temper. Now I think more about the consequences and I do not want the relationship with me and the person to become bad. If the person dies tomorrow and I fight and never say sorry, I will feel bad. So now, I say sorry for every little thing. I just want good relationship with everyone (Suri, F, 22).[96]

The study also revealed that the bereaved were seeking closer spiritual connection with God. Most of the youths shared that they strove and yearned to be nearer to Allah after parental death. A large majority shared that they were more serious about learning how to pray properly.[97] Finally, the study revealed that the youths were re-examining their spiritual selves. It was for them a time for spiritual reframing. Through this spiritual reframing, the youths obtained spiritual comfort in the knowledge that Allah cared about their parents and that was why he took them away.

The finding revealed that the youth also engaged in other ways of coping that were problem-focused: seeking social support and seeking practical diversions. Finally, the youths engaged in emotion-focused coping including ignoring the problem, keeping to oneself. The researchers recommended that future studies should be conducted to examine the influence that religion and spirituality play in the coping strategies employed by youths from different cultural groups.

From the study it can also be learned that grief experience is transformative because it integrates the spiritual and cognitive dimensions. The experience of death triggers deep reflection about life and about God, and this critical reflection leads to self-introspection which changes one's perception about life. A time of grief can be a time for systematic theology reflection (think about God as one ponders issues related to death and God) and practical theology (one seeks closer spiritual communion with God and re-examines one's life). This reflection on God and life mixed with

---

95. Ibid., 47.
96. Ibid., 48.
97. Ibid.

a deep self-re-examination leads to revival or a spiritual reframing. This is comparable to Mezirow's stage of perspective transformation.

There are other ways spiritual transformation can take place in people's lives. One of the ways is through integrating faith and learning in their education. It is in this perspective that a study was conducted by Lawrence, Burton and Nwosu to assess student perceptions of the faith-learning integration process in instructional methods courses taught by a single professor.[98] The study was guided by the question, "What are the students' perspectives of integration of faith and learning and the locus of behavior associated with integration activities?" This question was further elaborated on in three sub-questions:

(1) How do students define integration of faith and learning?

(2) Did the integration of faith and learning actually occur?

(3) Is integration a teacher behavior or a student behavior?

The research found that, regarding the understanding of integration of faith and learning (IFL), the majority of students defined IFL in connection with instruction (learning process, making connections in class, class atmosphere, etc.). Concerning the students' perception on IFL, it seemed that students had a high association of integration with teacher behavior or responsibility. Students were seen less often than teachers as the ones who were associated with integration activity. For instance, only three descriptions out of twenty-nine placed the student, rather than the teacher, in the active role. Finally, there was strong evidence that students believed integration was occurring. Only 3% said no and 85% said yes.

The study concluded with the recommendation that there was need to put more attention on the learning process so that students would be able to integrate their faith into whatever topics they are learning. To do this, Christian educators should develop the students' perspectives of integration of faith and learning and the locus of behavior associated with integration activities.

The researchers suggested cooperative learning and active learning strategies which could enable students to learn as they think and discuss, and as they provide the gauge by which the instructor determines if the right learning has occurred. In addition, the researchers suggested the use of overt demonstration, modeling and practice of how to think critically

---

98. Lawrence et al., "Refocusing on the Learning."

Theory of Education for Holistic Transformation

about issues and how to find resonance with their faith. In addition, they suggested the use of case studies for more mature students.

We would now like to turn to literature explaining how transformation takes place. Lawrence, Burton and Nwosu have given us a hint about the need for cooperative and active learning to foster transformative learning as the teacher integrates faith and knowledge.[99] Many other studies have been done to prove that community learning promotes transformative learning more than the traditional individualistic learning methods.

SOCIAL/COMMUNITY TRANSFORMATION

Social or community transformation is an important domain for Africans given the disparity between the existing resources and the real life of Africans which is largely characterized by poverty. The educational system that Africa has inherited from the colonial powers did not give Africans skills to transform their communities. Africans were not empowered to become self-reliant. So, what is empowerment, and which educational methods could empower Africans to see the reality of the problem and to tackle these problems so that they may achieve sustainable development?

Kabeer defines empowerment as a process that refers to the ability of individuals and community groups to see their own goals and to act collectively upon them as well as the ability to make their own choices.[100] In order to be empowered, Africans need to be able to be aware of their problems first. Second, they need to be able to reflect on these problems and propose different alternatives to come out of them. Finally, they need to critically evaluate the different alternatives and come up with the right choice that should lead them to a better situation.

For her part, Albertyn sees empowerment as a multidimensional concept that occurs in individuals on three levels: the micro or personal level, the interface or interpersonal level, and the macro or socio-political level.[101] Albertyn therefore suggests that facilitation of the process of empowerment in any development effort should take cognizance of these levels.

Speaking about the interrelationship among the three levels, Albertyn, Kapp and Groenewald state that once the individual feels personal

---

99. Ibid.
100. Kabeer, "Resources, Agency, Achievements"; Kabeer, "Gender Equality."
101. Albertyn, "Increased Accountability."

empowerment, he/she moves to feelings of control on the interpersonal and macro-level of empowerment.[102]

Speaking about methods for empowerment, the authors advise that in facilitating empowerment with a group of disempowered and marginalized people, focus should be put on the individual as being central to the process and trying to diminish the difference in power between the facilitator and the participants. Referring to Freire, Kolb, and Percy,[103] Merwe and Albertyn point out that in the case where education does not encourage questioning of inequitable social structures and assumptions that are distorted, the marginalized remain in the state of false consciousness, where they do not have a critical understanding of the reality of their circumstances. The challenge is thus to employ an educational approach whereby they can reflect and analyze their lives in participatory circumstances and create knowledge through the transformation of experiences. Learning in this case does not only take place on a cognitive level but also on a conative and affective level. In this case, participants do not learn as a result of information that is imposed on them but also enter in deep enquiry and questioning about their own knowledge and assumptions that might be distorted. Mezirow describes distorted assumptions as "assumptions that limit insights and openness to other ways of seeing themselves and other people."[104] Also, Mezirow explains that distorted assumptions can be psychological, sociolinguistic or epistemological.[105]

Psychological distorted assumptions are related to the way individuals view themselves; these include fear, inhibitions, locus of control and psychological defense mechanisms. Sociolinguistic distorted assumptions are related to the interaction with people based on that individual's cultural background, expectations, norms, and language. These can be related to ethnocentrism, egocentrism, social norms, and rules. Epistemological distorted assumptions refer to the way individuals are aware of knowledge and how they are using it.

The authors encourage the use of emancipator teaching methods for learning to be transformative. This is because critical thinking, self-reflection, dialogue and consciousness-raising facilitated in participatory

102. Albertyn et al., "Patterns of Empowerment."

103. Freire, *Pedagogy of the Oppressed*; Kolb, *Experiential Learning*; Percy, "Contribution of Transformative Learning Theory."

104. Mezirow, *Transformative Dimensions of Adult Learning*, 118.

105. Ibid.

Theory of Education for Holistic Transformation

circumstances, facilitate the process of transformation and enable participants to move from awareness of issues that confront them on a daily basis.[106] And to encourage critical thinking, self-reflection, dialogue, consciousness and participation, it is important to apply participatory learning methods where participants are actively involved. Techniques such as role-play, brainstorming, case studies, critical incident analysis (participant's description of an incident that is evident in his or her life) and metaphorical analysis (the use of metaphors to describe the experience of participants) encourage active participation.[107]

In a study, Merwe, and Albertyn report on an intervention for previously disadvantaged women staying in low-cost housing in a rural informal settlement.[108] Many of these women experienced the negative effects of powerlessness due to the political history of the area as well as the position of women in a rural community in Calvinia, a rural town in the Northern Cape Province in South Africa. The target group was a group of 15 women between the ages of 25 and 40 years who lived in government-subsidized houses.

The three different types of distorted assumptions (psychological, socio-linguistic and epistemological) were used as the theme topics for interpretation.

It was noted by observing journal entries that the most distorted assumptions were identified in the first three sessions. The non-distorted assumptions declined after session four and were more prevalent as the course progressed. This seems to indicate that participants responded in the beginning to questions without questioning their individual assumptions.

The study concluded with the advice that when working toward facilitating transformation in groups, it is important to be aware of the process and continuum of empowerment and to work systematically at enhancing individuals' skills by reflecting on their circumstances and acting accordingly. The emancipatory method challenges educators to go beyond the mere teaching of knowledge and skills and focus on participation, dialogue, critical thinking and consciousness-raising, which should eventually lead to transformation.

As stated earlier, learning is not holistically transformative until it transforms the learner and equips him or her to transform his or her

---

106. Ibid., 153.
107. Ibid., 154.
108. Merwe and Albertyn, "Transformation through Training."

community. Generally speaking, true transformative learning should have impact on individuals, families and communities. The study that was conducted by Bennetts in this regard was based on a large study of the Second Chance Trust (SCT).[109] The study addresses one major finding of transformational learning and its effects on 197 individuals, their close relationships, and their communities. The SCT offers money to those over the age of 30 in South West England to effect change within their lives for the benefit of their wider community. Mentoring support was available from the administrator, and fellows were encouraged to use that service. However, the responsibility was mainly on fellows themselves to initiate contact in accordance with the principle of self-reliance. This reflected well Mezirow's understanding of the aim of adult education which is to promote self-directed learning and, therefore, equip adults to better recognize that they are agents in their own lives and future.[110] Individuals evaluated transformative learning by the extent of major changes in thinking, feeling, acting, relating, and being.

Significant change was noted by 156 fellows and their responses formed six categories:

(1) Self-transformation;

(2) Coping with / instigating change in self and others;

(3) Transformed relationships;

(4) Increased educational drive;

(5) Career improvement; and

(6) Quality of life. Self-transformation appears to manifest from learning events that have had a deep impact on Fellows' beliefs, attitudes, behaviors and personae.

This study supports Mezirow's theory of perspective transformation.[111] Over the years people came to believe that change was possible, necessary and rewarding. They were inspired, gained new skills and were empowered, and their transformation affected the society in terms of how they acted and thought. Economic empowerment, if done within a transformative learning philosophy, can be holistically transformative, empowering the needy, and equipping him or her to impact his or her family and his or her

---

109. Bennetts, "Impact of Transformational Learning."

110. Mezirow, "Critical Theory of Adult Learning."

111. Ibid.

EXPERIENTIAL LEARNING

Hedin describes what experiential learning is, its methods and its model.[112] Hedin quotes Yount, who defines experiential learning as "active participation of learners in events or activities which leads to the accumulation of knowledge or skills,"[113] and Lewis and Williams: "Experiential learning comes from experience or learning by doing."[114] Furthermore, Usher and Solomon see experiential knowledge as "a key element of discourse which constructs experiences in a particular way, as something from which knowledge can be derived through abstraction and by use of methodological approaches such as observation and reflection."[115] Etling categorizes experiential learning into informal, non-formal and formal processes.[116] Informal experiential learning is described as incidental learning and everyday experiences, often learning "on your own." Non-formal experiences are planned by instructors and include goals, but are less structured and occur outside of formal educational settings. These are activities such as service-learning projects, internships, etc. Formal experiential learning is connected to classrooms in schools and universities, occurring in classrooms or laboratories, projects, and hands-on activities. Often described in comparison or in opposition to traditional methods in which the teacher's role is to "give" information to the student, with knowledge transmission as the goal of teaching, experiential education has been discussed, described, and debated as "an alternative and/or an enrichment to instruction and a philosophy."[117] The two distinctive features of experiential learning are (a) engaging the learners directly in the phenomena related to their studies, and then (b) requiring them to reflect on the experience, analyzing it and learning from it.

---

112. Hedin, "Experiential Learning."
113. Ibid.; quoting Yount, "Experiential Learning," 276.
114. Hedin, "Experiential Learning," 5; quoting Lewis and Williams, "Experiential Learning."
115. Usher and Salomon, "Experiential Learning," 161.
116. Etling, "What Is Non-Formal Education?"
117. Cantor, *Experiential Learning*, 1.

For instance, a university offering a degree in community development could partner with World Vision or Compassion International to allow students to have internships in local projects managed by these organizations, inviting staff from these projects to come to class and share practical issues regarding community development, or work on a common research project in which the university, the non-government organization of local people would be involved.

One of the ways to foster such experiential learning would be through Community-Based Participatory Research (CBPR). CBPR is a research method rooted in a community, serving community interests, encouraging citizen participation and geared toward affecting social change.[118] Advocates of community-based participatory research suggest that it is now time to increase collaboration across and between communities and universities.[119] CBPR would be the best way to go about this type of collaboration. CBPR is an approach to research that can be traced back to two distinct historical research traditions: action research and participatory research. Both action research and participatory traditions place an emphasis on meaningfully involving stakeholders in applied social research. Both traditions are concerned with problem-solving and change. And both traditions are focused on building stronger partnerships between academics and communities.

SUMMARY

This chapter expounded a theory of holistic transformation. The literature involved in the construction of the theory has revealed that the goal of transformative learning is to develop a critical awareness so that individuals can take action against the oppressive elements that hinder their growth, therefore becoming more authentic and useful. The core of transformative learning is critical reflection, which allows an individual to reflect on his or her assumptions as well as others' assumptions. The process of critical reflection is set in motion by a disorienting dilemma, such as triggering situations (death, loss of job, etc.) or other new experiences.

The theory of holistic transformation has also revealed that Mezirow's transformative learning has moved beyond the cognitive to include the affective, spiritual, and intuitive, as well as the community dimension, in our case. In any dimension of transformative learning, the theory has revealed

118. Greene et al., "Metaphor and Multiples."
119. Flicker et al., "Ethical Dilemmas."

that relationships are the most powerful catalysts for transformative learning. However, to be empowering, these relationships should be approached in a balanced power between the facilitator and the learners.

Four key issues in this chapter emerging from the reviewed literature in relation to the theory of holistic transformation are worth noting. First, most of these studies have suggested transformative learning to be conceived beyond the cognitive domain: It is holistic.[120] Second, relationships are at the core of transformation.[121] Third, the community aspect, although explained differently from the African concept, was mentioned in several studies.[122] Finally, some studies were clear that the goal of transformation is growth into authenticity.[123]

Given the context of Africa, it is suggested that we add to the existing elements of transformative learning, that of community transformation. Bennetts's study revealed that individuals' transformation can affect their families and entire communities,[124] while Merwe and Albertyn's indicated that in transformative learning learners express distorted assumptions during the first session, but as they gain awareness of reality, they develop in self-understanding and reflect on distorted assumptions.[125]

The studies related to the domain of education in Africa have revealed some important gaps that this study is going to fill. The study will be conducted among a population that was born and raised in Kenya, who speak a language other than English at home but use English in class, who went to school locally to learn from a curriculum that did not consider their informal and non-formal education received in their families as important, and which did not, generally speaking, prepare them to critically wrestle with and address their community problems.[126] These people are Christians who are now struggling to bring change in their families and communities.

---

120. Duerr et al., "Survey of Transformative and Spiritual Dimensions"; Murshidah and Kalyani, "Grief Experience"; Lawrence et al., "Refocusing on the Learning."

121. Wighting and Jing, "Relationships"; Zhao and Kuh, "Adding Value"; Selzer, "Effectiveness of a Seminary's Training"; Martin and Trueax, *Transformative Dimensions of Mentoring*; Webber, "Development of Cognitive and Affective Trust."

122. Merriam and Ntseane, "Transformational Learning in Botswana."

123. Fetherstone and Kelly, "Conflict Resolution and Transformative Pedagogy"; Freeman et al., "Do Learning Communities"; Adkins-Coleman, "I Am Not Afraid."

124. Bennetts, "Impact of Transformational Learning."

125. Merwe and Albertyn, " Transformation through Training."

126. Kingsbury, "Barriers and Facilitators"; Wolhuter and Steyn, "Learning from South-South Comparison."

Education for Holistic Transformation in Africa

This study will bring new insights that will prove useful in understanding the state of education in Africa today. Also, given that these people went to graduate schools and learned through a British curriculum and are now serving in their communities, they constitute the right population to evaluate in regards to whether their graduate education was transformative, relevant, and contextualized.

These studies have confirmed the need for approaching transformative learning in a holistic way (beyond the cognitive and including the spiritual, affective and communal dimensions). The review has also revealed that relationships are at the core of transformation and that the goal of transformation is growth into authenticity. Unfortunately, apart from one study conducted in Botswana in Africa,[127] all the other studies were conducted in the West. This study being based upon a grounded theory research, it is going to offer cultural insights into holistic transformation in the Kenyan context and also the particular experiences the graduates will have gone through that brought transformation in their lives and empowered them to serve their communities.

Finally, the fact that the sample will be made of an equal number of the two genders, and that all the sampled population will be Christian from two different environments of learning, one Christian and another public, will also provide insights on what is common to Christian students who do their graduate studies either in a Christian or public university. The findings will give insights on what the Christian universities could learn from public universities and verse versa in terms of preparing their graduates for holistic transformation.

Does the Bible support these ideas of transformation? How does this transformation take place? The following chapter of theological integration will answer these questions based on the study of Acts 2 which focuses on the pedagogical insights in Peter's sermon that led to the salvation of 3,000 people on the day of Pentecost.

---

127. Merriam and Ntseane, "Transformational Learning in Botswana."

4

Biblical and Theological View of Holistic Transformation

WHAT IS TRANSFORMATION?

The empirical research the author conducted for his doctoral degree involved 23 graduates from two Christian and two public universities in Kenya. In that study, the analysis of participants' data defined transformation as "a discovery that takes place when one's eyes are opened by a truth, experience or inner reflection."[1] These three avenues of thought occur either separately or simultaneously within an encounter with the different other.

Let's take the occurrence of truth. As you may have noticed, it is natural for us human beings to always tend to bring our assumptions into our interpersonal and intercultural relationships. When people build arguments on personal beliefs or assumptions, their conclusions could lead to ethnocentrism, a myopia that prevents us from seeing value in others' cultures. But when we encounter the truth, this new truth opens our inner eyes to a reality that we previously ignored, neglected, or simply did not know about. After such an encounter, we are therefore able to differentiate between assumption and truth.

Most of ethnocentric beliefs are based on assumptions, not on truth. It is an assumption to put people in one box and say, for example, "Black

1. Ntamushobora, "Exploration of Education."

people are lazy," or, "White people are imperialistic." When we encounter the different other, we get an opportunity to test our assumptions. Once we know the truth, it changes our old assumptions. We become free, for freedom is to know the truth (John 8:32). We then adopt a new perspective which is different from the old one. That is transformation!

So, how about a new experience? Anyone knows by their own experiences that a new experience can also transform us. An African proverb says, "He who has not travelled thinks that his mother is the best cook." I thought that African food was best, but while traveling in the United States, I've eaten Mexican and Asian food—and I've loved them; I have been transformed by these experiences.

Finally, regarding inner reflection, there are situations that have made me think twice about my beliefs, and as a result I have been changed through introspection. For instance, teaching undergraduate teenagers at Biola University has made me reflect more about parenting, and I have come to appreciate my children more than ever before. I have come to notice that teenagers are the same across cultures, and that I was more rigid on my children than I should have been. Teaching teenagers from another culture has transformed my parenting style.

These examples show that transformation takes place when our mind is awaken and begins to think anew. This new realization and freshened perspective becomes a new discovery. I call this discovery *eureka*.

According to Barbara Friberg and Neva Miller, the word *eureka* comes from the Greek verb *eurisko*, which means "a spiritual or intellectual discovery gained through observation, reflection, perception or investigation."[2] This is the reason why exposure to the different other is such an essential part of deep transformation, for it offers an opportunity to *discover*.

An example is when we talk with people who have visited new places. Returning travelers have opportunities now to compare what they knew before the trip with what they discovered while on their journey. I have heard many people who travelled to Africa say that they were amazed to see African Christians rejoicing even though they had so few possessions. This discovery is transformative; for these travelers saw how the deep pulse of God's joy is not tied to how much a person owns.

During my time in the United States, I also found that most Americans are not emotionally attached to an organization as they are to an individual. They want to connect with "Faustin and Salome" instead of being

2. *Analytical Lexicon*, s.v. "eurisko."

Biblical and Theological View of Holistic Transformation

connected to Transformational Leadership in Africa (TLAfrica, Inc.), with which they serve. This is a discovery that has transformed me and has affected the way I think about fundraising. I am now aware that Americans want to hear about my life, my story, my experiences, and my feelings far more than basic information about our programs in Rwanda, Congo, Burundi and other countries. They want to hear about the specific story of a widow in Rwanda and whose life has been transformed by a cow she received from TLAfrica, Inc., rather than the general statements about the organization, even if these are also important.

As Christians, when we are reading the Bible and come across a passage that is triggering, we tend to pause and think about it. We reflect on it, or consult a friend or dig it up in a Bible commentary to get the answer. As we discover more about the passage, the scripture comes with transforming power because it was not part of us before. That is why transformation is a succession of discoveries that build upon each other. These new experiences bring clarification to what we already knew, expand our knowledge, and challenge our faith. As Christians, it is those daily discoveries in our lifelong journey with the Lord through his inspired Word and fellowship with him and our fellow believers that change us into Christ's likeness. This is why I encourage believers to venture into reading the whole Bible, even books, like Song of Solomon, that people shy away from.

Another triggering experience could be a testimony that challenges the listener to think and ask questions. My testimony about transformation through suffering has helped believers who are frightened of hardship. After hearing my story, many people have told me, "Faustin, your testimony has challenged my resistance of moving from my comfort zone." A new testimony, especially one that doesn't fit with our cultural or personal concepts of the way God works, can make us uncomfortable. We start to ask ourselves if we have projected personal values onto God, and in this way, others' stories shake off the chaff in our souls, and help us press into a grace that surprises us in its many forms and faces. Encountering the different other helps us hear different stories and testimonies, which can in turn make us reflect on what that means for our personal lives and situations. And this kind of reflection changes our lives.

But *eureka* could also be triggered by a shocking observation or a provoking thought. One shocking observation I have made from my life in the United States is that while Africans are a community that is characterized by shame, Americans are not. When I would walk through Biola's campus,

I saw young people kissing each other, and people took it as normal. If you visit Uganda Christian University or Daystar University in Kenya, you would never see young people kissing each other in public. It is shameful. This shocking observation has transformed my cultural anthropology. I now take it as acceptable, even if I do not endorse it. I can now say, "It is okay for young Americans to do so," but I wouldn't have been able to say this five years ago. Interaction with Americans has changed my perspective. My new perspective is that it all depends on the heart's motivation. Young people not kissing each other in public may be doing terrible things in private.

Also, transformation can be triggered by a provoking thought. This was one way Africans mentored young people. If a father wanted to provoke his son to begin thinking about marriage, he would, for example, call the son and tell him, "You know so and so, son of so and so; do you know that you were born the same season, when we were harvesting corn? Do you know that if your friend dies today his name would remain? But if you die today your name would not. Go and think about it."

Jesus used provoking thoughts in his teaching. For instance, in Mark 2:1–13, Jesus told the paralytic man, "Son, your sins are forgiven." That was provocative for the Pharisees who were present. Eventually, they thought in their hearts that what Jesus said was blasphemy. Jesus, knowing what they were thinking, confronted them on the spot and demonstrated his authority by healing the paralytic. In verse 12, the healing of the paralytic "amazed everyone and they praised God saying, 'We have never seen anything like this!'"

In all of the above situations, the truth, knowledge or experience brings newness in one's thinking, feeling, beliefs and relationships with self, others and God. Let me illustrate this with my own experience.

When on December 19, 1979, after I heard a sermon from 2 Corinthians 5:17, I discovered that I was a sinner and decided to put my faith in Christ. I became a new creation. This newness heralded new thinking, feeling, belief and relationship with myself, others and God. From that day onward I understood the difference between being in Christ and in a religion. Previously, I was in a religion that made me enjoy meeting others on a Sunday, and singing in the choir with other young boys and girls.

But after the new experience, I understood that to be in Christ meant to surrender one's self to him for total control. Also, from that day onward

Biblical and Theological View of Holistic Transformation

I felt peace in my life. I accepted myself as I was. As I continued to read the Bible, I felt more freedom to live the Christian life. Before then, reading the Bible was a burden. I now felt more joy to live a life without the pleasures of the flesh that come with the addiction of sin. Furthermore, my beliefs changed. Before my salvation, I was shy to confess a weakness. But after salvation I found that confessing is not a weakness, but a strength that comes from the work of the Holy Spirit in my heart.

Ultimately, my salvation had implications for my relationship with myself, others and God. I accepted myself as I was more than I could do before, but also I began to see others as created in God's image, as sinners who can be forgiven as I myself was forgiven. Finally, I began to put God first in my life and follow his guidance rather than following my impulses.

HOW DOES TRANSFORMATION TAKE PLACE?

This section aims at exploring biblical insights about methods that could facilitate such transformation. Many biblical studies have been done to explain what transformation is (Rom 12:1–2; 2 Cor 3:18; Eph 4:17–24; Col 3:1–17), but fewer are the biblical studies explaining how this transformation takes place. This chapter is based on the study of Acts 2 and it aims at understanding the pedagogical methods that Peter used in his sermon on the day of Pentecost that led to the salvation of three thousand people, and how these new believers continued to be transformed.

THE EVENT OF THE COMING OF THE SPIRIT

The scene is the day of Pentecost, as the 120 disciples are gathered in one place. It seems it was a public place because soon a crowd was quickly drawn to the event. Pentecost was a Jewish festival that fell fifty days after the first Sabbath after Passover (Exod 23:16; Lev 23:15–16; Deut 16:9–12). It was also known as the Feast of Weeks or Feast of Harvest.[3] Luke pictures the event in a way that has an element of visibility to it, as vv. 2–4 make it clear. Its supernatural origin is also obvious, for what he describes came out of heaven. The roots of the promise of the coming of the Spirit are in the Old Testament (OT), such as in Numbers 11:29; Isaiah 44:3; and Ezekiel 36:27.

---

3. Kistemaker, *New Testament Commentary*, 95.

The first indication that something is taking place is the sound like a rushing wind filling the room where the disciples are seated. The Spirit's presence brings the manifestation of tongues. The distribution of these tongues among the believers is compared to a spreading fire, which divided up into bits of flame for each person (the theme of fire is something associated with divine activity, such as in Isa 5:24). It also suggests the power of God's presence. All those who were present were filled with the Spirit and spoke in tongues as the Spirit gave them utterance.[4]

Peterson explains that at Pentecost the disciples were "empowered, inspired and equipped for what would be essentially a verbal ministry."[5] According to him, the "other tongues" in the Pentecost event were intelligible languages different from their own, not the sort of tongues mentioned in 1 Corinthians 12–14, which could only be understood if someone interpreted. And so, for Peterson, "it was not simply a miracle of hearing: it was a miracle of speech."[6] Kistemaker explains that the word tongue used in Acts 2:6 is equivalent to the concept of spoken language.[7] Acts 2:6 says that "each one heard them speaking in his own language." So, when the disciples spoke in other tongues declaring the wonders of God (v. 11), these tongues were understood by their hearers.

In vv. 12–13, all who heard the praises of God in their own languages were amazed and perplexed. They could not grasp what was going on, and so they kept asking one another, "What does this mean?" Some, hearing their own languages spoken by one disciple and various other languages being spoken by the rest, made fun of them (mocking, sneering). They dismissed the disciples as having had too much wine. It is this attack against the disciples that prompts Peter to explain the event and proclaim Christ as Lord in his sermon that won more than 3,000 new believers to Christ.

TRANSFORMATIVE PEDAGOGY IN PETER'S SERMON

The purpose of Peter's sermon was to bring his hearers to salvation by repenting from sins and putting their faith in the Lord Jesus Christ. Repentance is the core step toward biblical transformation. It could be compared to perspective transformation in social transformative learning theory.

4. Bock, *Acts*.
5. Peterson, *Acts of the Apostles*, 134.
6. Ibid.
7. Kistemaker, *New Testament Commentary*, 77.

Biblical and Theological View of Holistic Transformation

According to Taylor, "A perspective transformation often occurs either through a series of cumulative transformed meaning schemes or as a result of an acute personal or social crisis."[8] Theologically, after one's old assumptions have been shaken, one feels sorry about his or her former ways. Peterson states that the OT regularly shows that repentance of sin involves an alteration of attitude towards God that brings about a "conversion" or "reorientation of life."[9] That is what we see in Acts 2:41. Those who opted for a reorientation of life by the way of repenting from their sins were three thousand. Repentance means a deep and radical change that affects the whole spiritual nature and involves the entire personality, including the intellect, the emotions, and the will.[10] We will see below in the exegesis of v. 37 that repentance here also includes faith. We thus have a picture of the way Peter shared the gospel of salvation that led his hearers to repentance and faith in the Lord Jesus Christ.

Preaching Truth Changed Thoughts: 2:15–35

Fulfillment of God's promise and Joel's prophecy: 2:15–21

Those who dismissed the disciples as having had too much wine were doing so on the assumption that speaking in tongues was for drunkards. Marshall explains that "this would be a very natural explanation to offer if one heard people making unintelligible noises, as some of the sounds must have seemed to those of the hearers who did not recognize the particular language being used."[11] Although this could have been a genuine thought, it was not the right thought. Peter offers the right explanation, that what happened was the fulfillment of what was promised by God long ago and confirmed by John the Baptist and Jesus in their time. Also, the prophet Joel had predicted that the coming of the Spirit would happen as an eschatological event, before the coming of the great and glorious day of the Lord.

---

8. Taylor, "Transformative Learning Theory," 6.
9. Peterson, *Acts of the Apostles*, 154.
10. Bromiley, *International Standard Bible Encyclopedia*, 136.
11. Marshall, *Book of Acts*, 71.

The risen Christ is Messiah and Son of David: 2:22–31

The Jews believed in Jesus' miracles but considered Jesus to be a kind of a magician, or a sorcerer (Luke 11:15). Josephus mentioned later that Jesus "was a doer of remarkable or strange works."[12] First, Peter demonstrated that Jesus was not a sorcerer but a man accredited by God himself. His explanation was to shake their wrong assumption by demonstrating that the signs that Jesus performed were divine; they were indicators of God working in and through him (Acts 10:37–38). Second, Peter demonstrated that it was impossible for death to keep Jesus because of what David spoke about him. David knew that God had promised him on oath that the Lord would place one of his descendants on his throne. Peter's point was that only through resurrection from the dead could a son of David rule forever over God's people. Strauss explains Peter's argument in a syllogism form:[13]

> Speaking in the first person, David predicted that the Lord's "holy one" would not see corruption (vv. 25–29); The death and burial of David, and the presence of his tomb in Jerusalem show that he had not fulfilled this prophecy (v. 29); David must therefore have been speaking of another. The natural conclusion is that David, knowing that God had promised to place one of his descendants on his throne, spoke prophetically of the resurrection of the Christ (v. 30).

The resurrection demonstrated that Jesus was the Messiah, who fulfilled a complex of Jewish hopes. He was the Savior-King of David's line, who reigns forever over God's people, bringing the blessings of forgiveness and peace with God.[14] Peter was the right person to give such a transforming teaching after he himself and the other disciples had had the same wrong assumptions immediately after Peter's confession that Jesus was the Christ, the Son of the Living God (Matt 16:21). When Jesus announced to his disciples that he was going to Jerusalem to die on the cross, Peter and others could not believe that. It seemed unfathomable that the "Son of the living God" could die. Furthermore, it was inconceivable that the One who was about to redeem Israel and set up the kingdom of David could be put to death. However, as Jesus explained, the Messiah must first suffer and then enter into his glory (Luke 24:26; 1 Pet 1:11). Peter is therefore giving

---

12. Bock, *Acts*, 120.
13. Strauss, *Davidic Messiah in Luke-Acts*, 140.
14. Peterson, *Acts of the Apostles*, 150.

Biblical and Theological View of Holistic Transformation

the same explanation he himself received from his Master when he was in the same bewilderment his fellow Jews are now in on this day of Pentecost.

The risen Christ is the fulfillment of the prophecy: 2:32–36

Peter demonstrates that Jesus was Messiah even before death. Since the Messiah was to rise from the dead, and since Jesus rose from the dead, it follows that Jesus was already the Messiah during his earthly life.[15] As a result of the resurrection of Christ, Jesus was exalted to the right hand of God the Father. Peter is therefore telling his listeners that "Jesus, seated at the right hand of God, has the authority to commission the Spirit to come and live in the hearts of the believers."[16] The coming of the Spirit is what the audience sees and hears. Thus, the Spirit's pouring fulfills the promise pointing to the last days and to the Messiah's mediation of salvation from God's side.[17]

Jesus' position makes him mediator of blessings of the Spirit and salvation: 2:34–35

Most of the Jews believed that no person was able to sit permanently in God's presence. God's glory and person are too unique to allow this. Bock points out that "the observation that Jesus has gone to God's side, although it is expressed figuratively since God does not have a limited location or a right hand, led to a high Christology, since it raises the question of who can sit in God's presence?"[18] According to Bock, this description of Jesus' position suggests an intimate connection between Jesus and the Father and equality between them.[19]

Changed Thoughts Awaken Emotions: 2:37–41

At this point, Peter's sermon has convinced the Jews that they are sinners and that they have crucified the innocent true Messiah. The truth has

15. Marshall, *Book of Acts*; Bock, *Acts*.
16. Kistemaker, *New Testament Commentary*, 101.
17. Bock, *Acts*, 131.
18. Ibid., 134.
19. Ibid.

now awakened the emotions. In verse 37 we read that the crowd was cut to the heart. Bock explains that *katenygēsantēnkardian* (cut to the heart) is an expression that appears only here in the New Testament (NT). The verb *katanyssomai* means to cause a sharp pain or a stab, often associated with emotion.[20] The Revised Standard Version (RSV) says the hearers were "acutely distressed." The New Living Translation says that Peter's words "convicted them deeply." The verb covers a range of emotions in the OT: anger (Gen 34:7); silence (Lev 10:3); having sorrow (Gen 27:38). It is used in the writings of Homer of horses stomping the earth with their hooves. Luke's remark about the heart shows the sincerity and depth of the audience's response.[21] Elliot points out, "Emotion serves to direct our attention and influence our thoughts . . . An emotion caused by cognition will exert influence on the cognitive process, and the chain will continue."[22] The crowd was moved by Peter's clear demonstration of the truth that what was happening was the fulfillment of the promise of God and that the one they had crucified was the Messiah. Peterson does not mince his words when he says, "When the people discovered how stubborn and foolish they had been, they were cut to the heart."[23] This reinforces the fact that emotion was caused by cognition. The truth that Peter declared (not the declaration per se) convinced the audience and disturbed their emotions so that they wished to know what to do. They therefore asked Peter and the other apostles, "Brothers, what can we do?" (v. 37).

The Greek word *poiēsomen* used in v. 37 is from the verb *poieō* which means "to do, to perform, to execute, to practice."[24] Gaventa comments that in Acts 2:37 the audience interrupts, but the interruption moves the sermon to its final appeal rather than stopping it entirely.[25] The crowd asks, "Brothers, what shall we do?" One can place this question at the center of the saving faith journey, considering that this journey is "a holistic engagement of the mind and heart that allows us to anchor theoretical and praxis knowledge to our faith—theoretical knowledge generating the concept-driven faith, and praxis-knowledge, the experience-driven faith."[26] So, once

20. Ibid., 140.
21. Ibid.
22. Elliot, *Faithful Feelings*, 47.
23. Peterson, *Acts of the Apostles*, 154.
24. Moulton, *Concordance to the Greek Testament*, s.v. "poiēsomen."
25. Gaventa, *Acts of the Apostles*.
26. Kim, "Cognitive and Faith Formation."

Biblical and Theological View of Holistic Transformation

the audience heard and understood the truth that the Christ whom they crucified was Lord, they were ready for a different direction, but they did not know which one. Thus, they asked the question, "What can we do?"

Bock comments, "The crowd is convinced and wishes to know what to do. Moved by an emotional and ethical concern, they sense the need to respond to this message."[27] The truth of the Word of God that Peter preached stirred their emotions and now they are willing to do something. Some of these people asking Peter what to do could have been the people who mocked Peter and other disciples when they were speaking in tongues saying they had too much wine (Acts 2: 13). Transformation begins when a person becomes authentic. To be authentic is to accept one's condition. Until one accepts that he or she is a sinner, no change can take place in his or her life.

Bock explains that spiritual formation has four key components: an agent (the Holy Spirit); a dynamic (growth in the context of community identification); a goal (holiness in the context of mission); and an open and responsive heart that pursues formation as a key purpose.[28] It seems that at this point the Spirit of God—the agent of transformation—was actively working in the lives of the hearers to bring them to conviction of their sins and to encourage them to repent.

In v. 38, Peter replies to the question of the disturbed hearers. He exhorts them to repent and thereafter to be baptized. The verb *metanoēsate* ("repent") is in the imperative mode and aorist tense. According to Dana and Mantey, "The imperative mode expresses the appeal of will to will."[29] Peter was appealing to the will of his hearers to repent. Dana and Mantey explain further that the aorist tense expresses "an action in single perspective and may be represented by a dot."[30] Peter was appealing to the will of his hearers to repent there and then and accept as true this Jesus whom they had despised and rejected.

But what is the meaning of repentance? Unger explains that *metanoia* ("repentance") means a fundamental and thorough change in the hearts of men from sin toward God. Although faith alone is the condition for salvation (Eph 2:8–10; Acts 16:31), repentance is bound up with faith and inseparable from it, since without some measure of faith no one can truly

27. Bock, *Acts*, 141.
28. Bock, *Acts*.
29. Dana and Mantey, *Manual Grammar of the Greek New Testament*, 174.
30. Ibid., 179.

repent, and repentance never attains to its deepest character till the sinner realizes through saving faith how great is the grace of God against whom he has sinned.[31]

Unger further describes the elements of repentance.[32] First, repentance involves a genuine sorrow toward God on account of sin (2 Cor 7:9–10; Matt 5:3–4); second, it involves an inward repugnance to sin necessarily followed by the actual forsaking of it (Matt 3:8; Acts 26:20); finally, repentance leads to a humble self-surrender to the will and service of God (Acts 9:6). In calling his hearers to repent, Peter is therefore commanding them to turn from their sinful ways and believe in the saving work of Jesus whom he has proclaimed to them.

Awakened Emotions Lead to Change of Will and Action

After Peter exhorted the hearers to repent and be baptized in the name of Jesus (as a testimony that what is believed in the heart is expressed visibly), about three thousand people accepted Peter's message and repented, turning to Jesus Christ for the forgiveness of their sins. The Greek word *apodechomai*, which is used in v. 41, means "to receive with hearty assent; to accept with satisfaction." Peter did not force anyone to repent. Repentance was done from everyone's will, with the help of the Holy Spirit convincing each one of his or her sins. The moment they made that voluntary decision, something new was done in their lives: that is salvation which begins with the new birth, continues with sanctification and culminates with glorification.

The new believers were baptized. Baptism is here a symbol of what has already happened in the heart of the new believer. Gundry explains that "getting baptized symbolizes in outward fashion the inward change of mind that repentance consists in."[33] Baptism, therefore, means a public declaration that the believers made to declare the change that had taken place in their hearts. Baptism for those who accepted Christ as Savior and Lord on the day of Pentecost did not achieve their salvation. Rather, it was an external vindication of their internal transformation.

---

31. Unger, *New Unger's Bible Dictionary*, 1072.
32. Ibid.
33. Gundry, *Commentary on the New Testament*, 472.

Biblical and Theological View of Holistic Transformation

FROM SALVATION TO SANCTIFICATION: 2:42-47

Peter's sermon has convicted 3,000 people who have repented from their sins and put their faith in Jesus Christ. They are baptized as public testimony of what has happened within their hearts. They have begun an eternal journey that will make them grow in the likeness of Christ their new Lord and Savior until they meet him in the time of glorification. This long journey has begun with a very important step, that of salvation. So, what is salvation and how will these newly saved people grow in the likeness of Christ?

Salvation

The Greek word *sōzomenous* ("those being saved") which describes the new believers in Acts 2:47, comes from the verb *sōzō*, which means "to save." Salvation in the Bible is the result of a saving act of God. This is true in both Testaments and in all aspects of salvation, from national deliverance to personal redemption.[34] To be saved is to enter the kingdom of God and to inherit eternal life (Luke 18:18-30). Eternal life as presented in the New Testament is not mere endless existence, for even those unsaved will never cease to be (Matt 18:8-9). Eternal life begins when one is saved from sin which came in the world through Adam, the first man and which separated mankind from God.

Salvation is man's restoration of his relationship with God through the second Adam, Christ, who died on the cross to redeem man (Rom 5:19). Through the first Adam, man is dead in sin. In other words, man is out of fellowship with God. But through the second Adam, man's relationship with God is restored. To live is, therefore, to relate to God and enjoy fellowship with him. Wright points out that "the salvation that the Bible talks about is holistic. It addresses the depths of the human person and the breadth of human society. It spans the realms of the physical and the spiritual; the past, the present and the future."[35] Wright's observation is important for this study that explores holistic transformation. Christ transforms not only individuals but also cultures and societies. Transformed people should therefore manifest fruits of salvation not only in the way they relate

---

34. Bromiley, *International Standard Bible Encyclopedia*, 288.
35. Wright, *Salvation Belongs to God*, 35.

with God and other human beings, but also in the way they transform their communities as part of God's Kingdom.

Transformation as Sanctification

After the Gospel (truth) had produced a paradigm shift in the life of the hearers who became believers of Jesus Christ, they needed to continue to be transformed in Christ's likeness. This process is called "sanctification." This is a progressive work of God and man that makes us free from sin and like Christ in our actual lives.[36] From this definition we can understand that sanctification is a cooperative venture between God who sanctifies and the believer who is being sanctified, and both God and man have roles to play. On God's part, sanctification by the Spirit includes his wise leading (Rom 8:1–6), purposeful discipline (Heb 12:3–13), powerful protection (1 Pet 1:5), and transforming freedom (2 Cor 3:17–18), among many other sources. On the other hand, Christians respond to God's work in their lives by yielding to the work of the Holy Spirit (Rom 6:13; Eph 5:18), reading, studying, memorizing, meditating on Scripture (John 17:17), praying (Eph 6:18), engaging in a local church (Heb 10:24–25), etc.[37] So, how does this process occur? We would like to examine some triggers of spiritual transformation in Acts 2.

1. **The Word of God**. The truth that cut to the heart of the Pentecostal believers was the transforming Word of God that Peter communicated effectively. So, it was not the method that challenged people, but the truth itself. The truth exposed the hearers to the reality of who they were and found themselves naked and needy for forgiveness. Saucy explains that "without an awareness of our spiritual ills, we would never seek God."[38] But even after they understood the truth and put their faith in Christ, they needed to continue to grow in Christ. As Saucy puts it, "Our new birth is the starting point of a continuous process of growth in a new kind of life."[39] That is why those who accepted Christ devoted themselves to the apostles' teaching (v. 42). They always met together in the temple courts (v. 46) to hear the apostolic preaching.

---

36. Estep et al., *Theology for Christian Education*, 214.
37. Ibid., 216–17.
38. Saucy, "Heart," 26.
39. Ibid., 7.

Biblical and Theological View of Holistic Transformation

Peterson states that "the earliest converts desired to be encouraged in their faith but also to identify with the public preaching of the gospel to their fellow Israelites as an act of testimony to its truthfulness."[40] One of the best books on transformation through the word of God is that of Richard Foster, *Life with God: Reading the Bible for Spiritual Transformation.*

In this book, Foster invites believers into a deeper and more authentic life with God. First, he calls believers to see the Bible afresh, because there are "millions of people who say that the Bible is the guide to life, but they still starve to death in the presence of its spiritual feast."[41] The author reminds us that knowledge of the Bible should lead us to greater appropriation of God's love for us and for us to have greater love for God, others, and ourselves.[42] Since the Bible is God's book, we must consider how we can ourselves come to it and also how we can present it to all people in a way that does not destroy the soul but inducts it into the eternal kind of life. This is not done through external conformity, but through the re-formation of the inner self of the spiritual core, the place of thought and feeling, of will and character.[43] This re-formation of the inner self happens when we read the Bible with understanding and with the heart. Reading the Bible with understanding involves reading it literally, in context, in conversation with itself, and in conversation with the historic witness of the people of God, while reading it with the heart, listening to the text of Scripture—really listening; listening yielded and still. That is what is called in Latin *lectio divina*, or divine or spiritual reading.[44]

Second, Foster suggests that to have the "with-God" life, believers should read the Bible with the heart so that they may acquire experiential knowledge of God.[45] To do so, believers should allow the Spirit to guide them as they read the Bible. This is so important because "the Bible is not a tool for sharpening our religious competences, but a living and active sword for cleaving our double-minded thoughts

---

40. Peterson, *Acts of the Apostles*, 160.
41. Ibid., 4.
42. Ibid., 7.
43. Ibid., 11.
44. Ibid., 15.
45. Ibid., 71.

and motives, exposing and transforming the contents of our hearts.[46] Also, the author suggests that in addition to reading the Bible with the heart, believers should read the Bible with the mind. This calls for reading with understanding. One danger of trying to understand the Bible is to take it only as a guidebook to religious life. The Bible rather is a collection of stories, all testifying to one grand story of a personal God in pursuit of relationship with human beings.[47]

2. **Prayer.** The word used for prayer in Acts 2:42 is plural with a definite article (*tais proseuchais*). It seems these were prayers in public worship services.[48] Peterson explains that the plural form with the article in Greek suggests that the reference is to specific prayer rather than to prayer in general. This most obviously points to their continuing participation in the set times of prayer at the temple (Acts 3:1). However, since their eating together in households involved praising God (v. 47), they doubtless also prayed in these groups, petitioning God about their own needs and the needs of others.[49] When believers came together they would hear the teaching of the apostles, fellowship over the Lord's Supper, share meals in homes, and unite their hearts in prayer. The question is, "How does prayer help in transformation?"

Prayer is important for transformation from the time of spiritual birth to the entire time of spiritual growth. In 1 Timothy 2:1–10, Paul exhorts Timothy to pray for all men, specifically for kings and all those in authority. In verse 4, Paul says that God wants all men to be saved and to come to a knowledge of the truth. Intercession thus has some spiritual effect in the salvation of sinners. In Romans 15:30–32, Paul says that prayer is part of spiritual battle. Satan fights believers from living in peace and from doing God's work. That is why believers are exhorted to pray continually (1 Thess 5:17).

Speaking about the role of prayer in spiritual transformation, R. L. Saucy states that the importance of prayer for our spiritual life and growth is found in the truth that it is in prayer where we most consciously live out our relationship with God—whether praise, thanksgiving, petition, or even lament. Saucy says:

---

46. Ibid., 75.
47. Ibid., 101.
48. Kistemaker, *New Testament Commentary*, 111.
49. Peterson, *Acts of the Apostles*, 162.

Biblical and Theological View of Holistic Transformation

In praise of our Lord we come to the real essence of human life. In our prayer of praise, we continually recognize and affirm our God for who he really is. In extolling the virtues of our Lord we are reminded of the greatness of his power and the immensity of his love for us. Praise is thus a rich form of meditation on God and our relationship with him—a great faith builder.[50]

As Saucy explains, "Prayers of petition likewise express consciously the truth of our dependent relationship on our Creator. Coming to our heavenly Father with requests is simply putting into practice our belief that all of our life—'every good and perfect gift' including our daily bread—comes from God (James 1:17)." Saucy further explains that "since our transformation takes place through a personal relationship with God, we cannot be transformed without prayer. In prayer we take God as real and personal. We become aware of his presence."[51] He therefore concludes that "to pray is to rise above the earthly realities of our life and connect with the ultimate level of our existence. Prayer is at the center of a personal relationship with God that transforms. As we participate in God's saving activity in the world through prayer, so it is through prayer that we participate in the 'working out' of our own spiritual transformation."[52]

Timms, speaking about the importance of prayer in our spiritual journey states, "Prayer draws us into the family of God and the community of believers. It motivates of holiness and the surrender of our own kingdoms. As our hearts grow more willing for the things of God, we find ourselves looking more to him for everything everyday and desiring his blessings with the impoverished."[53] But Timms goes further to explain how prayer moves our hearts to grow more willing for the things of God. He says, "As grace comes to us and pours through us we discover its radical power. And as we hold fast to faith in testing times and develop the discipline of resisting evil through confession and repentance, we experience life to the full."[54]

3. **Fellowship.** Fellowship is the translation of the Greek word *koinōnia* which generally means "something that is common." It also means

50. Saucy, "Heart," 295.
51. Ibid., 297.
52. Ibid.
53. Timms, *Living the Lord's Prayer*, 217.
54. Ibid.

"partnership" or "union" with others in bonds of a business partnership, a social or fraternal organization, or just proximity. In the New Testament, the words fellowship and communion are used interchangeably. They are both translations of the same Greek term *koinōnia*, from the verb *koinōneō*, "to share with someone something." *Koinōneō* thus implies two things:

(1) to have a share in;

(2) to give a share to.

The two implications call for another meaning applied to *koinōnia*, that of "participation."[55]

The spiritual meaning of "fellowship" / "union" has its foundation in fellowship and union/unity of the three persons of the Trinity. As Habermas puts it, "Christ calls his disciples into a life of relationship with one another that is modeled after the relationship of the triune God."[56] Habermas explains that "just prior to his death, Jesus prayed that his disciples would particularly experience the unity of godly fellowship: 'that they may be one as we are one' (Jn. 17:11)."[57] Habermas thus concludes that in Acts 2:44–45 *koinōnia* unity is described as a direct answer to Jesus' prayer.

So then, spiritual fellowship originates from the triune God; thus the heart of Christian communion is spiritual. By the Holy Spirit man communes with God and Christ, and the other saints. This communion arises out of the new birth (John 3:1–12), and is restricted to "those who are in Christ" (2 Cor 5:17). Their common spiritual paternity makes them one with common brotherhood (Heb 2: 11–13). This spiritual reality finds its source in the fact that Christ entered into a full fellowship of flesh and blood in order that he might thereby vanquish death. In 2 Peter 1:4, redemption is presented along these lines as liberation from the natural corruption of earth to participation in the divine nature. The whole church was included in Christ during his saving activity. This means that the church was united with Christ in his death and resurrection, and was made to sit with him in the heavenly places. This is called the mystical union between Christ and the believers, which is above any other form of fellowship among people. It should be noted that this union is personal. Every believer is personally united directly to Christ. Every sinner who is regenerated is directly

---

55. Robinson, "Communion," 752–53; Spencer, *Fellowship*.

56. Habermas, *Introduction to Christian Education and Formation*, 191.

57. Ibid.

Biblical and Theological View of Holistic Transformation

connected with Christ and receives his life from him (2 Cor 5:17; Gal 2:20; Eph 3:17–18).

Peterson remarks that "this sharing (described in Acts 2:42–47) was clearly a practical expression of the new relationship experienced together through a common faith in Christ."[58] The sharing of goods came to include the distribution of food to the needy in their midst (Acts 6:1–2) and was certainly not restricted to formal gatherings of the believers.[59] Peterson, therefore, advises that we should give *koinōnia* its widest interpretation in 2:42 including within its scope "contributions, table fellowship, and the general friendship and unity which characterized the community."[60] During fellowship believers praised and prayed together.

Whether disciples were together reading and studying the Word of God or fellowshipping together, or worshipping and praying together, all these were disciplines that were done from the heart and for each other. Their togetherness in studying the Word of God and their unity were strong triggers that could make them like Christ, for as they studied together, prayed together and fellowshipped together, their hearts were sharpening each other.

Proverbs 27:17 says, "As iron sharpens iron, so a man sharpens the countenance of his friend." The Talmud applied this verse to study: two students sharpening each other in the study of the Torah. It has, therefore, a direct application to two or more students (disciples) of the Word of God. The community of believers in Acts 2 was like a laboratory for experimenting and practicing what the apostles were teaching. This happened as disciples studied the Word of God together, lived together, interacted with one another, questioned each other, blessed and probably even offended each other. Let us use the analogy of an African sword that sharpens another to understand the usefulness of sharpening one another for spiritual transformation.

An African sword is kept in a scabbard so that it may remain sharp and does not harm anyone. It is drawn from its scabbard only when it is needed for use. Suppose that we have two swords that are kept in the scabbards—can these two swords sharpen each other? The answer is "no" of course. Even if one is removed from its scabbard but the other is not removed, the swords cannot sharpen each other. When the two swords are

---

58. Peterson, *Acts of the Apostles*, 160.
59. Ibid., 161.
60. Ibid.

removed from their scabbards, then they can sharpen each other without a problem. When sharpening each other, both swords get sharp and the bluntness is removed from each, maybe at different levels and times. Some bluntness may even require sharpening the sword several times.

From this analogy we learn the following lessons: First, unless the heart is removed from its scabbard, it cannot be sharpened. This means that unless there is trust between people who are fellowshipping, not much could be shared between them that could lead to transformation. Also, if only one person discloses and the other person does not, this could hinder true relationship development between the two and could hinder deep and continual transformation.

Verderber explains that people do not describe their feeling (do not disclose) as a result of one of the three assumptions.[61] First, people may believe that if they really tell their feelings they would reveal too much about themselves and so they would be vulnerable. Second, people believe that their feelings would in some way hurt other people. Finally, people may feel guilty about the feelings they have.

Icenogle explains that in dyadic or group communication, there are five levels of communication.[62] Level one is cliché conversation. This represents the least willingness to share myself with others. This is conversation that avoids engagement. Level two is about reporting the facts. This represents a minimal sharing of myself—a sharing of objective knowledge. Level three is that of sharing my ideas and opinions. This represents giving more of my individual and unique self. This demands more risk-taking on my part, for the other person has the potential to reject my idea or opinion. Much of human communication ends at this level. Level four is about sharing my feelings, values and emotions. These words represent my personal self. I am now speaking out of a more hidden part of my being. Level five is about confessional sharing. This represents peak communication. These are the experiences and feelings I may not ever share with another.

So, we understand why the heart is sensitive. Sometimes one may trust when the other has not yet trusted. Fellowship may take place but true transformation may still be hindered. As believers come together to study the word, fellowship, worship and pray together, they bring their intellect as well as emotion. Unless the two are engaged, the will may not be truly touched. In a community people may have different sorts of emotions: fear

61. Verderber, *Communicate!*
62. Icenogle, *Biblical Foundation for Small Groups.*

Biblical and Theological View of Holistic Transformation

of failing when asked a question, shame if one fails to answer a question during discussion, guilt of forgetting what one knows, pride resulting from knowing more than other people in the group, complex of inferiority or superiority depending on the position of the person in the group, etc. Yet, all these tensions are inescapable and are triggers for our transformation.

In African thought, the heart is the center of transformation, because it is the center of "human-ness." It is said that a man can have either "a heart of stone" (meaning that he does not have emotions such as empathy, love, care and does not think), or "a heart of a human being." Alex Kagame believed that the way of conceiving being in African philosophy is embodied in the "ntu" metaphysics that features four distinct categories in the Bantu thinking: *umuntu* (person); *ikintu* (objects); *ahantu* (place and time), and *ukuntu* (quality, relations). The person who has feeling (affective) for others or who understands (intellect) others is said to have the quality of human-ness that we call *ubuntu*.[63] The community is God's ordained school for shaping man's heart to grow into increasingly gaining more ubuntu. This goes with Saucy's definition that "transformation is nothing less than an increasing freedom from the power of sin's bondage in our daily experience of life."[64] In African terms, transformation makes us more "bantu." It is in the community that man's heart grows from a relationship with things (knowledge, information, objects) to a relationship with other human beings (self, others and God). To borrow from Kasyoka, one grows from an "I-It" relationship to an "I-You" relationship.[65] The former relationship cannot share the heart, for "It" cannot shape "I"; I can only be shaped by "You."

In conclusion, only life can shape life. This is the reason why relationship between "I-You" is more transformative than "I-It." "I-You" relationship leads to more understanding of who one is as one reflects on self through the mirror of the "You." For instance, it is in the community that the greatest commandment of loving God with all the heart and soul and mind and loving others as self is cultivated and developed. I can testify to this truth as a married Christian man, husband, and father. My wife and children have molded me into what I am today more than any information I have received from great mentors in my life. My heart has learned to be patient with my wife when she has delayed. I have learned to listen to her when she has expressed different opinions, and I have learned to listen to

63. Kombo, *Doctrine of God*.
64. Saucy, "Heart," 20.
65. Kasyoka, *Introduction to Philosophy of Religion*.

my children when they have complained against my many rules. Living among my family members has been a great school for my heart. That is the same for any community, especially for a Christian community of believers whose lives can sharpen each other using God's truth and wisdom. Saucy acknowledges that the normal spiritual growth or transformation of the believer takes place as the life-giving grace of Christ flows through the members of his body through their fellowship.[66] Explaining how this transformation takes place, Saucy points out, "In community we learn to live God's transforming truth together, gaining insight into its meaning from one another and being mentored in living it out in differing situations." He adds, "We get to know Christ through others and learn to live out the Christian story with them."[67]

SUFFERING AS ANOTHER TRIGGER FOR SPIRITUAL TRANSFORMATION

The review of literature of this study has already indicated that life crisis can serve as trigger for spiritual transformation. David Balk, Peter Bray, and Stanislav and Christina Grof all agree that life crisis events can challenge one's assumptions about human existence, therefore providing the ground for spiritual change.[68]

Experience shows that suffering and trials help us shape our theology—the way we understand who God is, our relationship with him, and our day-to-day life in this world. God uses this kind of school to mature us and to transform us into the image of his Son who also went through the same suffering. Also, God allows us to go through this kind of school so that once we mature in him, we may encourage others who are going through the same (2 Cor 1:1–5). Experience shows that the Christian's most profound and intimate experience of worship is likely to be in his darkest days—when his/her heart is broken, when s/he feels abandoned. Luke reports that despite persecutions during the early Christian church, the Word of God continued to spread, and the number of disciples increased greatly (Acts 6:7; 16:5). To mature our friendship, God will allow tests in our lives so that through periods of seeming separation our hearts may cultivate a

---

66. Saucy, "Heart," 230.

67. Ibid., 230.

68. Balk, "Bereavement and Spiritual Change"; Bray, "Broader Framework"; Grof and Grof, *Spiritual Emergency*.

Biblical and Theological View of Holistic Transformation

spirit of readiness for God's molding work. We may go through the dark night of the soul, but that will not mean that God has abandoned us, for he promises, "I will never forsake you" (Heb 13:5). He also promises in Psalm 30:5 that one may experience sorrow in the night, but joy arrives in the morning.

During times of suffering God acts as a refiner and purifier of silver. As a silversmith, he is however close to us in front of the fire the whole time the silver is being refined. Actually, he not only sits at the fire holding the silver, but he also keeps his eyes on the silver the entire time it is in the fire. If the silver was left a moment too long in the flames, it would be destroyed. When the silversmith sees his image reflected in the silver, he knows that the silver is fully refined.[69]

THE MAGNETIC POWER OF TRANSFORMED LIVES TO UNTRANSFORMED LIVES

Jesus' ministry was transformative because he offered personal attention to those he met. His life was the curriculum of his school. Jesus paid attention to children, women, sick people, lepers, Samaritans and Jews, and he approached everyone with dignity. He was interested to know the deep need of everyone, and to suggest a solution if the needy wanted it (he would ask for example, "Do you want to be healed?"). In this way, the unbelievers were attracted to him. Crowds of those who followed him were not all disciples; among them were those who were interested to know about this man whose life was different from others. Jesus' love, care and compassion coupled with his teaching became transformative in the lives of his disciples.

Coming back to Acts 2, verse 47 shows that the testimony of believers who were together, studying the Word of God together, fellowshipping and sharing their possessions with gladness attracted the attention of unbelievers who would be drawn to Christ. These unbelievers wanted to experience the gladness that was seen springing from the fullness of life that was expressed by the believers.

---

69. Ntamushobora, *From Trials to Triumphs*.

Education for Holistic Transformation in Africa

DOES ACTS 2 REFLECT HOLISTIC TRANSFORMATION?

As Smallbones recognizes, "Teaching for transformation begins with the realization that transformation is God's business and not our own, and lasting change is always the gracious work of the Spirit of God within, and often occurs despite the teacher's efforts."[70] For this reason, we can only observe indications of transformation that are factual. Spiritually, those whose old assumptions were challenged and who accepted the truth that Peter communicated were saved. They moved from darkness to light and from eternal death to eternal life. They entered into a new and unique relationship with Christ, the Messiah who died for their sins and who sent them the Holy Spirit who convicted them of their sins. But even after their salvation they continued to grow in the knowledge of the Lord Jesus Christ and his Word. They praised and prayed together; they went before the Lord with their petitions. Socially, they joined the disciples and formed a fellowship that was marked by love and unity. They met in their homes as well as in the temple. They shared meals together and celebrated the Lord's Supper together. This fellowship played a role in their transformation as they studied the Word of God together, ministered to one another, praised and prayed together. So, the social dimension of their life affected the spiritual. Economically, they shared their possessions and gave to everyone according to one's need. We can also deduce that the spiritual and social dimensions of their life affected the economic.

These three domains played a vital role in increasing the *phobos* (fear) in everyone's soul. This was not the kind of fear that we experience when something threatens us, but "a religious awe."[71] This awe was experienced by everyone. So, eventually even those who were not saved could have experienced this kind of awe. In other terms, the love and unity among the early believers produced more joy to live a holy life and at the same time it astonished the nonbelievers who were surprised by this extraordinary kind of life. The awe among the believers and nonbelievers was solidified by the fact that the apostles were performing visible signs. No wonder then every day some of these unbelievers who were struck by a sense of awe were being saved. It is, therefore, clear that the early believers' authentic life not only affected each other in the body of Christ, but it also had an impact in the community. As learning is concerned, they grew in their intellectual

---

70. Smallbones, "Teaching Bible," 295.
71. Witherington, *Acts of the Apostles*.

Biblical and Theological View of Holistic Transformation

knowledge as they continued to study the word of God; they increased in affective life through one another's ministry such as loving and encouraging each other; their sense of volition also increased as they put in practice the Word of God in their daily life. These elements are a clear indication that there was holistic transformation in the lives of the believers in Acts 2.

SUMMARY

The call to Christianity places us in the position of transformational agents where learning must be integrated with faith. For this to happen, a deliberate effort should be made to integrate the theory of holistic transformation with biblically and theologically sound principles. In this chapter I have attempted a biblical and theological integration of the theory of holistic transformation through the book of Acts 2. A close look at the theological findings from the study of Acts 2 shows similarity with the key issues noted in the studies that were reviewed on holistic transformation in chapter 3.

First, both the social science reviewed studies and the theological study of Acts 2 revealed that transformation takes place as a result of a triggering experience. This could be a crisis such as death,[72] or a change in one's perspective in terms of initial distorted assumptions.[73] The latter was the case for the Jews whose assumptions were distorted but later changed their perspectives after being convinced that the dead, buried and risen Christ was the one who sent the Holy Spirit on the day of Pentecost.

Second, both the finding from the reviewed social science studies and the theological findings from Acts 2 revealed that relationships constitute an important element that promotes transformation. These relationships could be experienced in a mentoring situation,[74] or in community responsibilities and relationships.[75] The theological study of Acts 2 was clear that the community life through fellowship and prayer for the early believers contributed much to their spiritual transformation. This was because, in addition to learning the transforming Word of God, they had an opportunity to sharpen one another by encouraging and learning from one another.

---

72. Murshidah and Kalyani, "Grief Experience."

73. Merwe and Albertyn, "Transformation through Training."

74. Selzer, "Effectiveness of a Seminary's Training"; Martin and Trueax, *Transformative Dimensions of Mentoring.*

75. Merriam and Ntseane, "Transformational Learning in Botswana."

Third, both the finding from the reviewed social science studies and the theological findings of Acts 2 revealed that emotions are important in transformation. For instance, the study by Fetherstone and Kelly found that cognitive trust was not significantly related to team performance while affective trust was significantly related to team performance.[76] In Acts 2, preaching truth changed thoughts of the hearers and these changed thoughts awoke emotions. When these emotions are aroused, they lead to change of will and action (repentance).

However, there is also a difference between social sciences and theology, and in our case the greatest difference is that social sciences attribute transformation to human agents (good teachers), or transformative experiences (for instance, trusting relationships increasing intrinsic motivation). While theology agrees with the social sciences to a certain point that a good teacher and good methods could lead to transformation, it posits that the ultimate source and agent of transformation is the Holy Spirit of God who works as catalyst during the communication process between the communicator and the receiver. The Holy Spirit is the one who causes transformation to take place in the mind and heart of an individual. Good teachers can help develop others' thinking, but they cannot change others' hearts. It is the Holy Spirit who transforms people's hearts through a supernatural new birth leading to everlasting life. Without this new birth in a person's heart, transformation is incomplete and not lasting. After the new birth, the Holy Spirit continues to work in a person's life until he or she reaches full maturity in Christ (Eph 4:13).

---

76. Fetherstone and Kelly, "Conflict Resolution and Transformative Pedagogy," 16.

5

Holistic Transformation in Africa
Findings from Research in Kenya

STUDY CONTEXT AND METHOD

The underlying purpose of this study was to explore the impact of learning experiences on the intellectual, spiritual, and community lives of Kenyan Christians who have graduated from master's programs from Christian and public universities. The study was exploratory in nature and utilized grounded theory research approach to understand the thoughts, experiences, and skills of graduates from two Christian universities (Nairobi International School of Theology and Africa International University) and two public universities (University of Nairobi and Moi University) as a result of their education in their former master's programs (appendix A). A grounded theory is an evolving method premised on the inductive generation of theory derived from data.[1] Its goal is to discover a theory that has a grab, would fit the data, and would work in the real world.[2]

The study was guided by the following research questions:

1. In what ways did learning experiences in master's programs impact Kenyan Christians' intellectual lives?

---

1. Stern and Porr, *Essentials of Accessible Grounded Theory*.
2. Ibid., 48.

2. In what ways did learning experiences in master's programs impact Kenyan Christians' spiritual lives?

3. In what ways did learning experiences in master's programs impact Kenyan Christians' community service involvement?

The study was conducted through semi-structured interviews (appendix B) which fit well within subjective theory. Here, subjective theory means that "the interviewees have a complex stock of knowledge about the topic under study (this knowledge includes assumptions that are explicit and immediate and which interviewees can express spontaneously in answering an open question)."[3]

A pilot study was conducted among three of the researcher's colleagues at Biola University who graduated from Nairobi International School of Theology and Africa International University. The pilot study helped test the internal consistency of the semi-standardized research questions before they were applied to the larger sample. A preliminary analysis of the data was done before the research questions were applied to the real research sample. The findings of the pilot study gave some insights on improving internal consistency of the research questions before field work.

A purposive sampling was used in this study. The case was based on a sample of graduate students because the topic dealt with higher education and at that level the graduate is able to think analytically and make some critical judgment in answering the interview questions. Also, these graduates are already mature and making a considerable contribution in the community. Therefore, they can evaluate how the training they received was transformative to them and relevant to their communities. The fact that the sample was made up of Christians only made it easy to learn from both Christian and public universities' unique contributions in holistic transformation in Africa. The same population category (Christian) which applied to both public and Christian universities was examined in light of various constructs of transformation (intellectual, spiritual, communal). That was because the researcher's interest was not in transformation of graduates from other religions, but only of Christians. The study assumes that without spiritual transformation, transformation cannot be holistic at all. Furthermore, it was assumed that data would give insights on the differences in transformation between males and females in both public and Christian universities.

---

3. Flick, *Introduction to Qualitative Research*, 155.

To obtain this sample, the researcher requested the administration of every university involved to help identify 10 Christian students, among whom five would be males and five females; students known for making a greater impact in their communities among the alumni who had graduated between June 2006 and June 2010 (appendix C). From the list of 40 graduates, the researcher selected 24 names of alumni using a stratified sample process divided equally between genders (appendix D). "Stratified sampling occurs when the researcher divides the population into subgroups (or strata) such that a unit belongs to a single stratum and then selects units from those strata."[4] In total, 23 Kenyan graduates from master's programs from two public and two Christian universities were interviewed.

Once data had been collected according to various stages, it was transcribed and the researcher proceeded to the theoretical coding. This is "the procedure for analyzing data, which have been collected in order to develop a grounded theory."[5] Coding means "the constant comparison of phenomena, cases, concepts, and so on and the formulation of questions that are addressed to the text. The analysis was done following the grounded theory method which is made of the following processes."[6]

The researcher used the NVivo (version 9) program to highlight the data into codes. NVivo9 program helped the researcher to organize the data in categories, themes and concepts. Woods explains that "categories are to do with basic properties; themes are unifying links running through wider spans of data; and concepts are ideas which elevate the data or parts of the data to a more theoretical level."[7] As the researcher went through the data highlighted by the NVivo9 program, he would discover new categories emerging from the data.

The next step of data analysis was to refine and differentiate the categories resulting from open coding. From the multitude of categories that were originated, those are selected that seem to be most promising for a further elaboration.[8] Flick explains that these axial categories are enriched by their fit with as many passages as possible. Finally, the relations between these and other categories are elaborated. Most importantly, relationships

---

4. Clark and Creswell, *Mixed Methods Reader*, 201.
5. Flick, *Introduction to Qualitative Research*, 296.
6. Ibid.
7. Woods, *Successful Writing for Qualitative Research*, 25–26.
8. Flick, *Introduction to Qualitative Research*, 301.

between categories and subcategories are clarified or established.[9] Flick points out that in axial coding the categories that are most relevant to the research question are selected from the developed codes and the related code notes.

The selective coding continues the axial coding at a higher level of abstraction. The analysis of axial codes was pushed further and the codes were reduced to 23 items forming 7 inter-related themes, all connected to one over-arching theme of "the other" as it will be seen in the following sections.

INTEGRATING FINDINGS WITH THE THEORY AND LITERATURE ON TRANSFORMATIVE LEARNING

On the one hand, the review of literature defined holistic transformation as a process of becoming critically aware of one's personal, historical, cultural, social, relational and spiritual contexts which lead to changing the assumptions and frames of references, resulting in perspective transformation of meaning which in turn empowers the learner to respond to his or her life circumstances with a wider repertoire of possible action. On the other hand, the respondents in the study defined holistic transformation as a new discovery, an eye-opener taking place in the life of a person who would see what he or she could not see before. This would happen as a result of some catalyst which played the role of changing the old way of seeing things into the new way. This catalytic experience would be triggered by a new revelation, new truth, a provoking thought, a shocking observation, or a new testimony. The whole process would take place in the intellectual, spiritual, affective, behavioral and communal life of the person.

Table 5.1: Comparing Literature Review and Findings

Reviewed Literature	Finding	Comparison
A process of becoming critically aware of one's contexts which lead to changing the assumptions and frames of reference	A new discovery, an eye-opener taking place in the life of a person so that the person would see what he or she could not see before	Similarity

9. Ibid.

Reviewed Literature	Finding	Comparison
The change would result in perspective transformation of meaning	The new way of seeing was called a new perspective	Similarity
Catalytic events such as life-crisis triggers (Balk, 1999; Grof and Grof, 1989)	The new perspective was triggered by a new revelation, new truth, a provoking thought, a shocking observation or a new testimony	Clarified
The perspective transformation of meaning empowers the learner to respond to his or her life circumstances with a wider repertoire of possible actions	This person with new perspective would exhibit change at the intellectual, affective, behavioral and spiritual levels	Similarity
	The process of holistic transformation takes place through the Holy Spirit, self reflection and "the other."	New finding from this study

Theoretically, the findings to this study confirmed Mezirow's three types of reflection: content, process and premise reflection.[10] Content reflection involves thinking back to what was done and, therefore, might involve a transformation of a meaning scheme; it is thinking about the actual experience. An example of content reflection could be the experience CHRUN2 who, through reading the Bible, came to understand God's revelation, too.

Process reflection is thinking about how to handle the experience. The best example for process reflection is that of CHRUN3 (see appendix D, "Third Respondent from a Christian University") who had to think about his vice chancellor's way of dealing with the problem that the class was experiencing. Although the vice chancellor knew the solution to the problem, he decided not to offer it. The vice chancellor rather threw the problem to the students, and that made CHRUN3 change his perspective on problem-solving. Here is the statement of CHRUN3:

> I remember my Vice Chancellor, one time we [the class] had a problem and he told us, "You know, the answer is with you!" And he left! That challenged me! I came to understand that I have the answer; I do not have to look for it somewhere else. (3, 5)

---

10. Mezirow, *Transformative Dimensions of Adult Learning*.

Finally, premise reflection requires the person to see the larger view of what is operating within his or her value system. It is examining long-held, socially constructed assumptions, beliefs about the experience or problem. This could be the case of PUBUN8 (see appendix D, "Eighth Respondent from a Public University") who came to understand that development in Africa is beyond what he used to think. It is a cluster of issues involving social, economic factors, and as he puts it, "all influencing development at the same time and there is need for an integrated approach to development" (2, 8).

Also, the finding revealed that the respondents' transformation stages were similar to Mezirow's process of transformative learning which begins with a disorientation of some kind, variously described as disruption of one's worldview, frame of reference, meaning perspective, or taken-for-granted assumption.[11] This leads to self-examination with others (in mutual dialogue), a critical assessment of internalized assumptions, and finally a perspective transformation or a new meaning perspective. Such was the case of CHRUN2 who could not understand why there are different denominations, but later on came to understand that all depends on the interpretation of governance in the Bible.

Compared to the reviewed literature about education in Africa, the findings are a true symbiosis between the Western formal education (*I* in relation to *me*; self-reflection; critical thinking) and the traditional African education system that promoted the communal way of life as a school in itself (transformation through the other person and for the other person). The latter goes in line with the review of literature and the theological integration that have confirmed that relationships are at the core of transformation and that the goal of transformation is growth into authenticity. This authenticity takes place as the self grows into becoming more like the Great Other who is the transformer par excellence. This growth comes as the self reflects on itself (*I* and *me*), and as the "self" interacts with the other (*I* and the *other*), whether familiar or unfamiliar. In all this process, the Great Other plays the role of catalyst and catalyzer.

Also, the findings showed the zeal, passion and cry of African graduates to see education in Africa using relevant and contextualized teaching methods and material. This could be a reaction of the current African elite to African colonial curriculum that was not relevant enough to the need

---

11. Mezirow, "Transformative Learning as Discourse."

Holistic Transformation in Africa

of Africans.[12] Contextualization in this study was defined as "bringing to life, every day's experiences so that the learners may see themselves in the picture, their villages, their neighborhood and their existential realities." This definition touches the core of the self; it touches one's identity. Contextualization could be a powerful way of transformation, and lack of it could also constitute a hindrance to transformation as the findings have revealed. Such a cry about the lack of contextualization as a hindrance for transformation can be heard in the following lament:

> One of the areas we lack is that of African scholarship; that is a very big deficiency. Most of the scholarly work that we used for our master's program was written by people from the western world which is not a problem or a sin, but I would have loved that I would have come across textbooks and references that were written by people who were coming from the African background, because there is a taste that you can't get when you read a book that is written by people from a certain orientation . . . (CHRUN11, 4, 1)

Speaking about transformative methods, the finding of this study confirms the general educational principle that for educational methods to be transformative, they should be relevant to the culture. As Lingenfelter puts it, "The cultural context of schooling is important for teachers at every level of education."[13] For instance, the review of literature indicated that the colonial (European) educational system in Africa promoted learning by reading books while traditional African educational methods promoted interaction with others. Most of the respondents indicated that they had been transformed through the other—either familiar or unfamiliar. This does not mean that learning through books did not have a place in their transformation. In fact, some participants stated that they were transformed through reading the Bible, books that were against their beliefs, or doctoral dissertations. The emphasis of being transformed more through the other than through written material goes with the concern that the respondents voiced about the non-contextual nature of written material and the fact that the respondents were more community-oriented than written literature oriented as seen earlier.[14] Actually, the dimensions of transformation

---

12. Kwabena, "British Curriculum Development"; Kelly, *French Colonial Education*.
13. Lingenfelter, *Teaching Cross-Culturally*, 17.
14. Ibid., 208.

as found in this study were closely related to the characteristics of the seven aspects of traditional African education as described by:[15]

Table 5.2: Comparing African Traditional Education with Study Findings

Characteristics of African Traditional Education (Fafunwa, 1982)	Findings: Education for Holistic Transformation
Develop physical skills	Not discussed (applied to younger persons)
Develop character	Spiritual transformation
Develop values: respect for elders and those in authority	Spiritual transformation
Develop intellectual skills	Intellectual transformation
Develop vocational training skills	Behavioral transformation
Develop a sense of belonging & participate in community	Affective transformation / community service involvement
Promote cultural heritage of the community	Missing point: The cry of most participants

Comparing the finding with reviewed empirical studies, the present study corroborated the empirical studies that highlighted the need for spiritual experiences that serve as triggers for deep reflection about life and God.[16] For instance, the study has revealed that trials were considered as times when respondents would come closer to God. PUBUN3 acknowledges that the challenges she went through during her master's program impacted her spiritually. She states:

> Sometime I would face challenges that really required me to come back to him [God]. Sometime I would lack some facilities. Despite that, I found that my education was a gift from God because I realized that there were many people we were together at undergraduate but they were not able to continue in their master's program. So, the program, apart from improving my intellectual abilities, it impacted on me spiritually. It made me realize that there was a force behind that. (2, 3)

In this case, PUBUN3 would reflect on her life and her relationship with God during the time of trials and would see God's blessings despite

---

15. Fafunwa and Aisiku, *Education in Africa*.
16. Murshidah and Kalyani, "Grief Experience"; Lawrence et al., "Refocusing on the Learning."

her challenges. Through her self-reflection, she would come to the conclusion that there must some spiritual power behind her success.

The finding for the present study also supported Bennetts's study that individuals' transformation can affect their families and entire communities.[17] Such was the case of several of the respondents who, after their master's programs, were involved in empowering their communities through direct projects such as the Village Tourism and Homestead project that was initiated by PUBUN5 in his Abagusii village, and many other respondents who sit on boards for schools in their communities.

Finally, the findings of the present study corroborated empirical studies that have confirmed the need for approaching transformative learning in a holistic way (beyond the cognitive and including the spiritual, affective and behavioral dimensions). The present study revealed that affective transformation could come as fruit of other dimensions. Data from the present study revealed that a person who is transformed intellectually and spiritually, and who is empowering his or her community, has a sense of fulfillment. It is this sense of fulfillment that motivates the person to seek more transformation because, as we have seen in the review of literature, awakened emotions lead to change of will and action.

COMPARING FINDINGS WITH BIBLICAL TEACHING ON TRANSFORMATION

The overarching theme of "the other" corresponds well with the biblical understanding of transformation through relationships.

First, "the other" in the African context implies inclusion. It is the "other person" who comes to extend "my being" so that I may be able to truly say, "I am because we are." This is different from the Western "the other" as coined by Gayatri Spivak which denotes "a relationship created by imperial discourse to connote an abstract and generalized but more symbolic representation of empire's 'other.'"[18] As seen earlier in the previous chapter, "Othering" in the Western context denotes some exclusion. However, "Exclusion of the 'other' simply because it is 'other' and different is foreign to Africa."[19]

17. Bennetts, "Impact of Transformational Learning."

18. Spivak, *Critique of Postcolonial Reason*, quoted in Ashcroft et al., *Post-Colonial Studies*, 156.

19. Setiloane, *African Theology*.

Education for Holistic Transformation in Africa

In the African biblical context, "I" needs "You" so that "I" and "You" can sharpen each other. The findings of this study have therefore confirmed that it is in community that the heart and soul and mind and loving God and others as self are cultivated and developed.[20] As Saucy pointed out, "We get to know Christ through others and learn to live out the Christian story with them."[21] Also, the finding has confirmed that the Holy Spirit is the "Great Other" because it is from him that true fellowship between "I" and "You" originates. As seen in our theological integration, "spiritual fellowship originates from the triune God." In fact, the finding corroborated Smallbones's statement that "teaching for transformation begins with the realization that transformation is God's business and not our own, and lasting change is always the gracious work of the Spirit of God within us, and often occurs despite the teacher's efforts."[22] No wonder all the themes were coded under the theme of the Holy Spirit, author of transformation.

Also, the study found that affective transformation was the feeling that graduates had as a result of the fulfillment in the other areas of transformation. In our theological integration study of Acts 2 we found that emotion helped in the work of salvation of the early believers. It was found from Acts 2 that awakened emotions led to change of will and action. But we can also see another level of emotion among the early believers during their phase of spiritual formation as they lived in community. They shared their possessions with others with joy, and their life was full of praise. This kind of life was the fruit of what was happening in their inner life. There seems to be an agreement between theology and psychology that affective domain (emotions) could be the fruit of fulfillment of the other domains—when a person understands the Word of God and puts it to practice, the result is joy in one's life.

In the same line of thought, the study found that the participants pointed out the behavioral transformation that had taken place in their lives was the result of the use of their spiritual gifts and talents, or the application of the other dimensions of transformation (spiritual, intellectual and affective) for the benefit of the body of Christ and community at large.

Finally, the literature review about transformation, the theological integration and the finding of this study have all confirmed that trials are one of the ways that triggered transformation in the life of a Christian (2

---

20. Ntamushobora, *Transformation through the Different Other*, 146.
21. Saucy, "Heart," 230.
22. Smallbones, "Teaching Bible for Transformation," 295.

Cor 1:1–5). For example, Balk and Grof and Grof indicated that life-crisis events could challenge a person's assumptions about the meaning of human essence.[23]

COMPARING GRADUATES FROM CHRISTIAN AND PUBLIC UNIVERSITIES

The finding revealed that one of the two Christian universities was doing better in mentoring graduate students than the other. Comparing graduates from Christian and public universities, the finding revealed that, on the one hand, although all had a heart to see their communities transformed, graduates from public universities were more proactive in rendering their services to the community beyond church initiatives. On the other hand, graduates from Christian universities understood better what transformation meant and seemed to be better prepared for their chosen career after graduation than those from public universities. This preparation was due to internships and mentoring that graduates from Christian universities received during their education. It also seemed that the curriculum for Christian universities was more structured with emphases and specializations more than the public universities. But all of the participants, whether from Christian or public universities cried for contextualization of the use of relevant curriculum and teaching methods.

INTEGRATING FINDINGS WITH RESEARCH QUESTIONS

This section revisits the three research questions (RQ) in chapter 1 that guided the study and answers them in relation to the research findings described in this chapter. To get data for these RQs, 11 interview questions were asked of 23 graduates from Christian and public universities in Kenya.

Intellectual Transformation

Intellectual transformation was first expressed in the answers about the definition of credibility as a reason for the choice of a graduate school. Six answers were given by graduates as reasons why they chose a school for their master's programs: credibility of the school, personal and family

23. Balk, "Bereavement and Spiritual Change"; Grof and Grof, *Spiritual Emergency*.

convenience, passion and alignment with a career goal, service to community, financial consideration and divine direction. Speaking about credibility, graduates from Christian universities meant a school that integrated academics and spirituality and which would give them skills for ministry. Graduates from public universities chose schools for master's programs because of their quality education, which depended on good human resources and facilities. From this starting point, it can be seen that intellectual transformation was one of the key motivations for graduates to choose a school for their master's degree programs.

Speaking about how learning experiences challenged the way graduates used to view life before, and how they think today as compared to the way they used to think before their master's program, respondents used themes of new perspective (new realization, eye opened), new understanding, expanded understanding to describe the intellectual transformation that took place in their lives as a result of their learning experiences in their master's programs.

In this study, perspective was used synonymously with "seeing." Change of perspective meant that one used to see through the old assumption, then something happened (triggering event) that made the person change the way he or she used to see and adopted a new way of seeing (a new perspective). The new way of seeing or new perspective could take place in one's mind for personal transformation (I saw learning in a different way), or in the way one viewed others for interpersonal transformation (I saw community in a different way).

New realization was also used synonymously with "eyes were opened." The new realization described well the "eureka" that took place in the life of the respondents. It is the new realization that would make the respondent say, "I have found; I have discovered the truth." When a respondent says, "I realized that without the right understanding of missions, most institutions will just exist for the wrong reason" (CHRUN10, 8, 1), it means that before she received the teaching on right reasons for missions, her eyes were blind toward the idea of what is the right reason for mission. But immediately after the professor or someone else explained what the right reasons for missions were, it was a "eureka." Her eyes were immediately opened. She got it! And that is what led her to a new perspective about missions. All the other themes related to intellectual transformation such as new understanding, new critical thinking, independent thinking and analytical thinking fall under the category of perspective transformation.

Spiritual Transformation

All three questions were related to spiritual transformation. Respondents stated that they had experienced spiritual transformation through spiritual experiences, expansion of their faith, more understanding of spiritual matters, and that their theological positions firmed up. But as noticed in this chapter, not much was said regarding spiritual transformation. As explained in the previous chapter, that could be due to the fact that graduates from public universities were not in their fields when expressing theologically their spiritual transformation. However, when it came to explaining the role of the Holy Spirit in their transformation, they all had things to say, even though not at the level of graduates from Christian universities. That could be due to the fact that "to the African, religion is like a skin that you carry along with you wherever you go."[24] An African recognizes that God is the giver of everything. He does not need necessarily to explain how God does it. It was easier therefore for participants to say what God did to "self" than explaining how "the self" was spiritually transformed.

The experiences that the participants shared about the role of the Holy Spirit in transformation varied from guiding one into choosing a school for the master's program to providing for tuition and other needs for life and family, giving intellectual ability to study and do well academically, providing encouragement in times of trials and many others. No wonder the theme of Holy Spirit came as overarching theme among all the seven themes of the study. All the other dimensions of transformation derived from the Holy Spirit. The Holy Spirit is the author of transformation and he is the one who catalyzes it. The Holy Spirit was called teacher. He is a teacher, guide, enabler and comforter (John 14:26). The work of the Holy Spirit was acknowledged by graduates from both Christian and public universities. PUBUN7, for example, a graduate from a public university said that the Holy Spirit gave him courage to challenge the superstitious beliefs of his people. The Holy Spirit's work was acknowledged in one's transformation as working in "the other" either familiar or unfamiliar for one's transformation. The Holy Spirit is therefore the one who works through the professor, fellow students, guest-speakers and others for the transformation of the learner.

24. Healey and Sybertz, *Towards an African Narrative Theology*, 25.

Education for Holistic Transformation in Africa

Community Service Involvement

From the beginning of the interviews till the end, it was obvious that participants viewed education as a tool for community transformation. When graduates were asked what motivated them to choose a university for their master's program, one of the reasons they gave was to be able to serve others. The theme of community service had two main categories: service to others and empowering others. PUBUN1 defined "empowerment" as "increasing the potential of people rather than bringing them development." Empowerment can be done by change of perspective as well as by economic empowerment. The study found that all the graduates were concerned about community change but did it in different ways. Graduates from Christian universities used their position in the church to serve their community. This was done through a school or any other project that was begun by the church. But some graduates from public universities, in addition to serving in the church, took personal initiatives to serve in community beyond the church entity.

Answering IQ9, participants gave several answers to the evaluation of their programs. Most of the participants were happy with the programs they went through, but they all cried for more contextualized material and subjects. They expressed the desire to see their schools offering education that is relevant to their people in terms of course contents and learning materials. Emphasizing the need for materials written by Africans, CHRUN12 stated that even if a *Mzungu* (white man) could write about Africa, there is still some African-ness missing in the writing. She explained it this way:

> I don't think even if we used African writers; maybe one or two! You know—maybe I have a bias—but I will tell you—even if a "*mzungu*" [white man] writes about Africa it is not the same as when an African writes about Africa. There is some African-ness missing in the *mzungu*—kind of. And I asked my teachers twice, "Where are the African writers?" (5, 5)

A HYPOTHESIS SUMMARIZING THE FINDINGS OF THE STUDY

The unifying theme that best explains the education for holistic transformation as explained by graduates from master's programs in Christian and public universities in Kenya seems to be the phrase, "Eureka by the Great

Other through the other and written material and for the other." Word frequency queries for the twenty most frequent words indicated that "people" and "God" were respectively the first and second most frequent nouns. Twenty-one out of twenty-three of the respondents pointed out that the Holy Spirit was the author of their transformation, be it spiritual, affective, behavioral or intellectual. Most of respondents would agree with CHRUN6 when he stated, "You cannot speak of transformation without mentioning the Holy Spirit because the Holy Spirit is the greatest transformer. He is the one who helped me get the transformation I needed. You cannot ignore his role even on the intellectual part. Intellectualization without the Holy Spirit can be frustrating." It is the Holy Spirit who sends light in the inner eyes of the person so that one is able to see what he or she could not see before. From this time onward, the person has a new perspective and thinks, feels, believes and acts differently. Although the Holy Spirit is a person, he is more than a person. He is the Great Other, for he is the author and catalyst of transformation.

The light that comes from the Great Other passes either through "the other" or some written material for one to receive it. Some participants stated that they were transformed through reading books or dissertations. Written material constitutes the basis for reflection in critical thinking. The same applies to self-reflection that comes through reading a book, such as the Bible. The Holy Spirit works through the written Word of God to transform the reader. However, majority of participants stated that they had been transformed through "the other." As said earlier, this reflects the communal worldview of Africans which value relationships above written materials. "The other" could be the self (self as object or "me" as opposed to self as subject or "I"), the other person (familiar or unfamiliar), or the Holy Spirit himself. Even when the respondents spoke about courses that brought more new perspectives in their lives, they had to mention the person who was behind the course.

Regarding the means by which *eureka* takes place in one's life, respondents stated that it was through "the other," written material, self-discovery and divine revelation. "The other" was defined as either the familiar other or the unfamiliar other.

The familiar other was mainly colleague students and professors. On the one hand, as professors taught in a transformative way, they challenged the learners to think and change their perspectives. As professors mentored learners through small groups and fellowships, learners were enabled to see further than they knew. As professors exhibited humility before their protégés, the learners became more humble. On the other hand, as learners saw their colleagues' commitment, they were challenged. As they heard different views from their colleagues, they came to appreciate diversity in culture and thinking. The same was said for participants who were challenged by listening to people from totally different views and opposing ideas which would make the participants think twice, even when they would not agree with the other people with opposing ideas.

In addition to being transformed through the familiar other, participants stated to have been transformed through the unfamiliar other. For instance, participants stated that interacting with colleagues from different denominations was eye opening. This transformation came as a result of learning to stop judging those from different denominations and appreciating them rather. Also, guest speakers were said to have challenged some participants. The visit of some renowned guest speakers would give an opportunity to learners to interact with them when it would have been difficult to reach them in other ways.

In addition to being transformed through the other—either familiar or unfamiliar, the participants stated that they were transformed through self-discovery. On the one hand, as participants made personal decisions; as they made introspections; as they became aware that they are limited in their knowledge and ignorant in many areas, all these were situations that made participants examine themselves and which led to their transformation. On the other hand, self-discovery also took place as participants made a shocking observation; as they accepted themselves as they were; as they appreciated their cultures and as they identified themselves with their people.

The transformation that the participants called *eureka* and the means that they described through which *eureka* took place were both aimed at not self-ambition, but serving the other in the community and helping him or her change his or her perspective. The former was done through initiating development projects for the community, serving on school boards and putting down one's ambitions for a good job out of the community just to live and serve among one's people. The latter was done through equipping the community members with the Word of God, mentoring other people, loving and accepting those who do not share one's opinion as one agrees to disagree in love. Implicitly, empowering and mentoring others could be done either through relationship or written material.

IMPLICATIONS FOR THEORY, RESEARCH AND PRACTICE

This study has implications for theory, research and practice as discussed below

Theory and Research

First, the study has added value to the theory of transformative learning in education by integrating the Western understanding of transformative learning with the biblical and African understanding of transformation. The study comes to support Taylor's idea that transformative learning has moved beyond Mezirow's dominant conception to include the spiritual and affective dimensions of transformation and to recognize the centrality of relationships in the transformative learning process.[25] This study has clarified how the intellectual, spiritual, affective, behavioral and communal dimensions are interrelated.

Understanding holistic transformation is helpful in Africa for educators, church leaders, social workers and community developers who all would like to see Africans transformed and empowered to change their communities. The time has come when Africans should bring transformation to their communities not because they are told to do so, or because they have heard it from others, but because they have "discovered" (*eureka*) that it is important for them and that they believe they can do it. It is this discovery leading to new perspective change that will lead to true dignity and authenticity of Africans.

Regarding the theory of transformative learning applied to Africa, this study could serve as an example for conducting other qualitative studies in Africa, so that a theory of education for holistic transformation may be developed in the future, based on findings from several countries and from several different educational systems (the systems in Kenya that were studied were British—for public universities, and British and American for the Christian universities). However, even now the findings give a hint,

25. Taylor, "Analyzing Research."

particularly for the four universities sampled in Kenya, and even for other universities in Kenya, of what education for holistic transformation in the African context looks like.

Practice

This study has given some more evidence that the African worldview has a great potential for changing people's lives. First, as it has been said, spirituality is embedded in the African worldview.[26] What people need is the right understanding of spirituality, and that is in the teaching of the Word of God. Second, the belief in a communal life is important for community change and the appreciation of the other person. In Africa, my humanness increases as I relate with "the other" who could be another person or God himself, the Great Other. This concept of the other, if well developed and practiced, could lead to peace and reconciliation, and could promote more development among Africans.

The study has indicated that the church remains the main venue for community change. The local church brings together people from all backgrounds so that they can serve each other. Both graduates from public and Christian universities pointed out that they had ministries in the church and that the goal of those ministries was to serve others. The church was also the venue for developing some projects that would bring change in communities.

RECOMMENDATIONS FOR EDUCATIONAL PRACTICE IN AFRICA

From the findings of this study the following are recommended:

First, we recommend that, in case it is applicable, educational efforts in churches and Christian schools in Africa should intentionally develop and apply learning objectives of teaching to personal and community levels.

Second, as Christianity continues to grow on the continent and the need for more transformation of communities continues to arise, we recommend that more educational efforts be organized to mentor and disciple those who are educated in disciplines other than biblical and theological so that they may be better equipped with spiritual foundations as they serve in

---

26. Healey and Sybertz, *Towards an African Narrative Theology*.

their communities. We also recommend that theological schools introduce into their curriculums more courses related to community service, so that graduates from Christian universities may be able to communicate with those from public universities whose backgrounds are at the same level of understanding. This would help non-theologians to be more involved in church ministry and the pastor-theologians to be more involved in community services even when these services are not directly related to church, but are a real need of the community.

It is in the same perspective that we also recommend that churches make more proactive moves to partner with universities in their surroundings so that Christian students in institutions of higher learning may be better prepared to serve in church and community with biblical worldviews. Most of the time, the work of equipping students in universities has been left to ministries such as Campus Crusade for Christ and others. Yet, after graduation these students meet in the local church, not in the ministry organization. It is therefore better for the local church to get in touch with students when they are still in training in university so that their service in church at graduation may be a continuation of a preestablished relationship between the students and the church. This could be done by the local church in partnership with the other ministries involved in campus student ministries.

Third, we recommend that graduate programs in universities in Africa develop some courses on writing and publication that are different from the normal courses on research methods. With the cry for Africans to have curriculums that are relevant and teaching material that is contextualized, there is need to intentionally train and mentor graduates so that they may be able to do that actual writing. We propose that such a course be done in an African mentoring format so that it does not give just information, but hands-on skills.

Fourth, we recommend that universities keep in touch with their alumni and consult them as the universities review their existing programs and as they develop new ones. The alumni who have gone through the curriculum of the alma mater and who are now practicing what they learned are in a better position to give feedback on proposed curricula and input on new courses to consider in the new curriculum.

Finally, we recommend that Christian universities make an international effort to disciple and mentor their graduates-in-training instead of assuming that they are mature and just need intellectual knowledge as it was found in this study.

LIMITATIONS OF THE STUDY

First, this was a qualitative study conducted among 23 graduates from four universities in Kenya. Although the findings give hints to what education for holistic transformation in Africa looks like, they only reflect the learning experiences of graduates from the four sampled universities. A larger sample would have therefore given more light in how education for holistic transformation in Africa looks like.

The second limitation was the use of only one research method, the semi-structured interviews. The use of a variety of research methods such as focus group discussions among participants or a longitudinal study whereby graduates could be interviewed before they begin their graduate programs and at the end of their programs in order to see how transformation would have occurred in their lives, could give more light in the transformation process of the research participants.

RECOMMENDATIONS FOR FURTHER RESEARCH

First, it is recommended that further research studies be initiated in other parts of Africa, preferably in non-British colonized countries so that the findings may be compared and that in the future Africans may come up with their theory of education for holistic transformation as they themselves understand it. Such a theory should be based on transformative learning theory and adapted to the African worldview and culture.

Second, it is recommended that the same study be duplicated in Kenya with one group of male graduates and another group of female graduates in order to examine how sex affects transformation in the African context. Such a study would be useful especially when we consider that African women are going through great cultural change. Women are sleeping giants in Africa, and to empower a woman is to empower a community as we saw in chapter 1 of this study. At the time of writing this dissertation, Africa has a woman president (Liberia) and many women who sit in parliaments. How they view transformation and how they would like to see their communities changed as opposed to men's views, could be an important consideration for both educators and other decision makers.

CHAPTER SUMMARY

The purpose of the current chapter was to review major findings of this study and relate them to the three main research questions in chapter 1, the theory of transformative learning and the reviewed literature in chapter 2, and the theological integration in chapter 3. It was seen that the unifying theme that best explains the education for holistic transformation as explained by the research participants could be the phrase, "Eureka by the Great Other through the other and written material and for the other." Most of the respondents pointed out that the Holy Spirit was the author of their transformation, be it spiritual, affective, behavioral or intellectual. The Holy Spirit worked through the other, self-discovery and written material to bring the light in one's inner life to produce *eureka* that opened one's eyes to see the world with new perspectives. This was done for the sake of helping other people change their perspectives and serving one's community in different ways.

Comparing the findings with the theory of transformative learning, the findings revealed that transformation is a new discovery that takes place through a new perspective, and that the new perspective is triggered by a new revelation, new truth, a provoking thought, a shocking observation, or a new testimony, and that the process of holistic transformation takes place through divine revelation, self-reflection and "the other."

Also, the study confirmed Taylor's idea that transformative learning has moved beyond Mezirow's dominant conception to include the spiritual and affective dimensions of transformation and to recognize the centrality of relationships in the transformative learning process.[27] The present study clarifies how the intellectual, spiritual, affective, behavioral and communal dimensions are interrelated.

Comparing the findings with the reviewed literature about education in Africa, the findings seemed to be a true symbiosis between the Western formal education ("I" in relation to "me"; self-reflection; critical thinking; transformation through written material) and the traditional African education system that promoted the communal way of life as a school in itself (transformation through the other person and for the other person). Also,

27. Taylor, "Analyzing Research."

the findings showed the zeal, passion and cry of African graduates to see education in Africa using relevant and contextualized teaching methods and material.

The study ends with recommendations for more educational efforts to be made to disciple and mentor students in universities in preparation for their service in the community with a strong biblical foundation, and for students in Christian universities to take more courses about the community service that would be waiting for them after graduation or even during their study.

Finally, the study recommends more studies to be conducted in other parts of Africa, especially in countries that use non-British curriculums, so that in the future a theory of education for holistic transformation may be developed, applicable to the greater part of Africa. The study recommends also that the same study be duplicated in Kenya with two groups of different gender in order to examine how gender affects transformation in the African context.

Appendix A
Description of Sampled Universities

MOI UNIVERSITY (MU)

Moi University is situated in Eldoret, Kenya. The University was founded in 1984 and offers degrees in bachelor's, master's and doctoral programs. The University offers courses in agriculture and biotechnology, arts and social sciences, business and economics, dentistry, education, engineering, environmental studies, human resources development, information sciences, law, natural medicine, resources management, public health and sciences. The main language of instruction is English and the library is of about 100,000 volumes. (International Handbook of Universities, 2010, p. 2, 118)

UNIVERSITY OF NAIROBI (UON)

The University of Nairobi was founded in 1956 as Royal Technical College of East Africa, under the British colony. It became University College Nairobi in 1963 and acquired the present status in 1970. The main language of instruction at the UON is English and the degrees that are offered range from bachelor's to doctorates. The University of Nairobi offers courses in arts and design, biological sciences, business, computing and informatics, dental sciences, education, engineering, external studies (Continuing and Distance Education), journalism and mass communication, law, mathematics, medicine, nursing, pharmacy and physical sciences. In addition to these majors, the University has several institutes: African, anthropology and gender studies; development studies; diplomacy and international

Appendix A

studies; nuclear science; and population studies and research. (International handbook of Universities, 2010, p. 2, 118)

AFRICA INTERNATIONAL UNIVERSITY (AIU)

AIU is a Christian chartered University in Kenya and it is the successor of Nairobi Evangelical Graduate School of Theology (NEGST). NEGST came into being through the vision of late Dr. Byang Kato of Nigeria who was at the time the first African General Secretary of the Association of Evangelicals in Africa and Madagascar (AEAM), now Association of Evangelicals in Africa (AEA). He was deeply concerned because at that time the evangelical churches in Africa had seen little need to provide training for their pastors beyond certificate or diploma level. Although Byang Kato died in December 1975, the vision he had begun continued. The first class of four students began their studies in October 1983, and in July 1986, NEGST granted its first four graduates the Master's of Divinity (M. Div.) degree.

On March 4, 2011, NEGST was turned into a University chartered by the Kenyan government and became the African International University with three schools, namely: Nairobi Evangelical Graduate School of Theology (NEGST), Institute for the Study of African Realities (ISAR) and the School of Professional Studies (SPS). Today, AIU offers two doctoral degrees in biblical studies and translation studies; a master's of philosophy degree in education; three master's of theology degrees in biblical studies, missions and world Christianity; six master's of divinity degrees in biblical studies, missions studies, Christian education, theological studies, translation studies and church history; eight master's of arts in biblical studies, Christian education, church history, missions studies, pastoral studies, theology, translation studies, and organizational leadership. In addition, AIU offers a bachelor's degree in theology and a diploma and certificate in Christian ministries (http://negst.edu/prospectus/leadin.htm downloaded on October 23, 2011).

NAIROBI INTERNATIONAL SCHOOL OF THEOLOGY (NIST)

The roots of the Nairobi International School of Theology (NIST) are entwined deeply in the philosophy and history of Campus Crusade for Christ International. Campus Crusade for Christ (CCC) began its work in East Africa in the early 1970s and by that time there was a need for a graduate level theological institution that would integrate the highest standards of academic

Description of Sampled Universities

excellence in the study of God's Word with the best, most practical methods of communicating the truth with a dying world. In September 1981, the first class of five students began. They graduated in June 1986 (http://wwww.nist-kenya.org/content/view/20/97 downloaded on October 23, 2011).

Today, NIST offers master's of divinity degrees in chaplaincy, Christian education and formation, counseling, biblical and theological, intercultural leadership studies and pastoral studies. NIST also offers two master's of arts in counseling and leadership, and three bachelor's degrees in theology, education in counseling and science in leadership and management.

Appendix B
Research Questions

OPENING QUESTIONS

1. Would you please share briefly about yourself?
2. What influenced you in the choice for a school to attain your master's degree?

TRANSITIONAL QUESTION

3. In what ways did your learning experiences in the master's program challenge the way you used to view life before you attended your graduate school? Please give an example.

RQ # 1: TL IMPACTING INTELLECTUAL LIFE

4. If you were to compare the way you think today and the way you thought before you entered your master's program, would you find that your level of thinking has stagnated, developed or regressed?
   a. Please explain how this happened?
   b. Please give an example to support your answer.

RQ # 2: TL IMPACTING SPIRITUAL LIFE

5. In what ways did your learning experiences in your master's program impact your spiritual beliefs and practice? Please give an example.
6. Would you share one spiritual experience that you went through as a result of your learning in your master's program?
7. As a Christian, what was the role of the Holy Spirit in all these experiences you have shared with me?

RQ # 3: TL IMPACTING COMMUNITY SERVICE INVOLVEMENT

8. In what ways did your learning experiences impact the way you are involved in your community today? Please give an example.

EVALUATIVE QUESTION

9. As you reflect on your learning experiences in your master's program:
   a. Which areas would you say your master's program addressed well in terms of your own transformation as an African and the transformation of your community?
   b. What do you wish your master's program would have covered in terms of your own transformation as an African and the transformation of your community?

CLOSING QUESTIONS

10. What would you recommend to the administrators of your alma mater to ensure that those who come after you will receive an education that is holistic and transformative?
11. In light of our discussions, would you please share any additional comments?

Appendix C
Letter to and Responses from Universities Sampled

Dear Vice Chancellor,

RE: Permission to obtain names and contact information of 10 alumni for the sample of my doctoral research

My name is Faustin Ntamushobora. I am a student in the PhD Educational Studies program at Biola University in Los Angeles, Southern California.

I am writing to request permission to obtain names and contact information of 10 Christian graduates (5 females and 5 males who graduated between June 2006 and June 2010). The topic of my research is: *From Transmission to Transformation: An exploration of Education for Holistic Transformation in selected Christian and Public Universities in Kenya.*

The purpose of my research is to explore the impact of learning experiences on the intellectual, spiritual and community lives of Kenyans who have graduated from master's programs in selected Christian and public universities in Kenya.

The finding for this study will help universities in Kenya in particular and Africa at large to improve their learning experiences and pedagogical methods for more transformative outcomes. In addition, the study will inspire other disciplines such as theology, community development, missions, etc. that use the term of holistic transformation without prior empirical study of what it means for Africans. Finally, it is our hope that the findings will

Letter to and Responses from Universities Sampled

inspire universities for the review and design of curriculum that is transformative and holistic.

Attached are the interview questions that I will administer to the selected graduates. For any other questions regarding this project, your office can contact me at: Faustin.Ntamushobora@biola.edu
I look forward to receiving a favorable response.

Faithfully,

Faustin Ntamushobora
13800 Biola Avenue
La Mirada, CA 90639
Tel. 562-903-6000 (USA)
Tel. 254-720-752-953 (Kenya)
E-mail: Faustin.ntamushobora@biola.edu

Appendix C

"Committed to His mission connected to His world"

24 August 2011

Faustin Ntamushobora
13800 Biola Avenue
La Miranda, CA 90639

Dear Faustin,

RE: PERMISSION TO UNDERTAKE RESEARCH

Receive greetings from Africa International University!

I acknowledge receipt of your letter requesting for permission to conduct research for a PhD thesis on the topic: *From Transmission to Transformation: An exploration of Education Holistic Transformation in selected Christian and Public Universities in Kenya.*

Your request is hereby granted. Please get in touch with our Registrar

Meanwhile we wish you success in your studies.

Yours faithfully,

Allan Mbugua
For Deputy Vice - Chancellor Academic Affairs
Africa International University

c. c. The Registrar

CONSTITUENT SCHOOLS:
SCHOOL OF PROFESSIONAL STUDIES (SPS) | INSTITUTE FOR THE STUDY OF AFRICAN REALITIES (ISAR) | NAIROBI EVANGELICAL GRADUATE SCHOOL OF THEOLOGY (NEGST)

Letter to and Responses from Universities Sampled

Nairobi International School of Theology

July 3, 2011

Faustin Ntamushobora
13800 Biola Avenue
La Mirada, CA 90639

Dear Faustin,

RE: <u>Permission for Masters Alumni Contacts for Doctoral Research Interview</u>

Following your letter requesting for permission to obtain alumni contacts from the Registrar's Office for your Research Interview, as discussed, the contacts are available to you since these are our alumni. The department of Development and Planning will advise you on the names of the alumni to contact after which yo can obtain the contacts from our office.

God's blessing as you carry out the research.

Yours Faithfully,

Rosemary Gitonga
Registrar

P. O. Box 60954 • 00200 • Nairobi • Kenya
Tel: 2720837/8 • Fax: 2720253 • nist@maf.or.ke
A Ministry of Campus Crusade for Christ

Appendix C

MOI UNIVERSITY
DEPUTY VICE CHANCELLOR
(RESEARCH & EXTENSION)
INTERNAL MEMO

FROM: Deputy Vice Chancellor (R&E)	DATE: 10th August, 2011
TO: Alumni Officer	REF: MU/DVC/REP/27B

SUBJECT: AUTHORITY TO OBTAIN NAMES AND CONTACT INFORMATION OF 10 ALUMNI OF MOI UNIVERSITY – BY FAUSTIN NTAMUSHOBORA

Mr. Faustin Ntamushobora is a Ph.D Educational studies programme at Biola University in Los Angeles Southern California. His research topic is *"From transmission to Transformation", an exploration of Education for Holistic Transformation in selected Christian and Public Universities in Kenya.*

It is noted that Mr. Ntamushobora would like to obtain names and contact information of 10 Christian graduates (5 females and 5 males) from a master's program who graduated between June 2006 and June 2010.

This is therefore to grant authority to Mr. Faustin Ntamushobora to access the request information.

Upon the completion of the interview, he is required to leave a copy of the report in Alumni Office.

Any assistance accorded to him shall highly be appreciated.

PROF. B. E. L. WISHITEMI
DEPUTY VICE CHANCELLOR
(RESEARCH & EXTENSION)

CC: PAO (Extension & Outreach)

Letter to and Responses from Universities Sampled

UNIVERSITY OF NAIROBI
OFFICE OF THE DEPUTY VICE-CHANCELLOR
(ACADEMIC AFFAIRS)

Telegram:	Varsity	Telephone: 0254-020-318262
Telex:	28520 Varsity KE	P.O. Box 30197-00100 G.P.O
Fax:	2214325	Nairobi
E-mail:	dvca@uonbi.ac.ke	Kenya
Website:	www.uonbi.ac.ke	

22 August 2011

Faustin Ntamushobora
13800 Biola Avenue
La Mirada, CA 90639.

Dear Mr. Ntamushobora,

PERMISSION TO OBTAIN NAMES AND CONTACT INFORMATION OF 10 ALUMNI OF UNIVERSITY OF NAIROBI TO SERVE AS SAMPLE FOR DOCTORAL RESEARCH

Further to the above, I am pleased to inform you that your request has been approved.

Yours faithfully,

B. M. WAWERU
AG. ACADEMIC REGISTRAR

BMW/fnm

ISO 9001:2008 CERTIFIED
The Fountain of Knowledge
Providing leadership in academic excellence

Appendix D
Profile of Interview Participants

No	Name	Gender	Age	Alma Mater	Major	Year of Graduation	Church/Denomination	Current Job
01	CHRUN1	F	50–60	NIST	MDV/Biblical Studies	2007	Baptist	Pastor
02	CHRUN2	M	30–40	NIST	MA/Leadership	2008	Non-denominational	Church minister
03	CHRUN3	F	40–50	NIST	MA/Leadership	2009	Pentecostal	NGO
04	CHRUN4	M	30–40	NIST	MA/Intercultural	2009	Pentecostal	Pastor
05	CHRUN5	F	40–50	NIST	MDiv/Leadership	2006	Baptist	NGO
06	CHRUN6	M	40–50	NIST	MA/Education	2010	Pentecostal	Pastor
07	CHRUN7	M	50–60	AIU	MA/Education	2006	Pentecostal	Pastor/teacher
08	CHRUN8	F	30–40	AIU	MA/Education	2007	Non-denominational	Church minister
09	CHRUN9	M	40–50	AIU	MA/Pastoral Studies	2008	Pentecostal	Pastor
10	CHRUN10	F	30–40	AIU	MA/Missions	2009	Seventh DA	PhD Student
11	CHRUN11	M	50–60	AIU	MA/Biblical Studies	2010	Pentecostal	Pastor/teacher
12	CHRUN12	F	50–60	AIU	MA/Education	2007	ACK	Pastor/teacher
13	PUBUN1	M	40–50	UNBI	MA/Project Planning	2009	United Methodist	Lecturer

No	Name	Gender	Age	Alma Mater	Major	Year of Graduation	Church/Denomination	Current Job
14	PUBUN2	F	20–30	UNBI	MA/Conservation Bio	2010	Friends Church	*Off. administrator*
15	PUBUN3	F	20–30	UNBI	MA/Linguistics	2010	AICA	Banking
16	PUBUN4	F	40–50	UNBI	MA/Communication	2007	Catholic	Government
17	PUBUN5	M	20–30	UNBI	MA/Development	2010	Catholic	NGO
18.	PUBUN6	M	40–50	UNBI	MA/Project Planning	2009	Catholic	Government
19	PUBUN7	M	30–40	MOIU	MA/Ecotourism	2008	Catholic	Lecturer
20	PUBUN8	F	40–50	MOIU	MA/Communication	2007	AIC	Lecturer
21	PUBUN9	M	30–40	MOIU	MA/Education Admin	2009	Pentecostal	Univ. administrat
22	PUBUN10	M	30–40	MOIU	MA/Education Admin	2009	Pentecostal	Univ. administrat
23	PUBUN11	F	30–40	MOIU	MA/English literature	2010	Catholic	Lecturer

Bibliography

Abidogun, Jamaine. "Western Education's Impact on Northern Igbo Gender Roles in Nsukka, Nigeria." *Africa Today* 54 (2007) 28–51.
Adeyemi, Michael B., and Augustus A. Adeyinka. "The Principles and Content of African Traditional Education." *Educational Philosophy and Theory* 35 (2003) 425–41.
Adeyemo, Tokunboh. *African Contribution to Christendom*. Nairobi: AEAM, 1982.
———. "Africa's Enigma." In *Faith in Development: Partnership between the World Bank and the Churches of Africa*, edited by Deryke Belshaw et al., 31–38. Delhi: World Bank and Regnum, 2001.
Adekunle, O. Dada. "Decolonizing Theological Education in Nigeria." *Doon Theological Journal* 6 (2009) 146–61.
Adkins-Coleman, Theresa A. "'I Am Not Afraid to Come into Your World': Case Studies of Teachers Facilitating Engagement in Urban High School English Classrooms." *Journal of Negro Education* 79 (2010) 41–53.
Akilagpa, Sawyerr. "Challenges Facing African Universities: Selected Issues." *African Studies Review* 47 (2004) 1–59.
Albertyn, Ruth M. "Increased Accountability through Monitoring Empowerment Programmes." *Journal of Family Ecology and Consumer Science* 33 (2005) 31–36.
Albertyn, Ruth M., et al. "Patterns of Empowerment in Individuals through the Course of a Life-Skills Programme in South Africa." *Studies in Education of Adults* 33 (2002) 180–200.
Analytical Lexicon of the Greek New Testament. Edited by Timothy Friber et al. Grand Rapids: Baker, 2000.
Ansell, Nicola. "Secondary Education Reform in Lesotho and Zimbabwe and the Needs of Rural Girls: Pronouncements, Policy and Practice." *Comparative Education* 38 (2002) 91–112.
Ashcroft, Bill, et al. *Post-Colonial Studies: The Key Concepts*. 2nd ed. New York: Routledge, 2000.
Balk, D. E. "Bereavement and Spiritual Change." *Death Studies* 23 (1999) 485–93.
Barkan, Joel D. *An African Dilemma: University Students, Development and Politics in Ghana, Tanzania and Uganda*. London: Oxford University Press, 1975.
Bassey, Magnus O. *Western Education and Political Domination in Africa: A Study in Critical and Dialogical Pedagogy*. Westport, CT: Bergin & Garvey, 1999.
Baur, John. *2000 Years of Christianity in Africa: An African Church History, 62–1992*. Nairobi: Paulines, 1994.

Bibliography

Bennetts, Christine. "The Impact of Transformational Learning on Individuals, Families and Communities." *International Journal of Lifelong Education* 22 (2003) 457–80.

Bock, Darrell L. *Acts*. Baker Exegetical Commentary. Grand Rapids: Baker Academic, 2007.

Bondy, Elizabeth, et al. "Creating Environments of Success and Resilience: Culturally Responsive Classroom Management and More." *Urban Education* 42 (2007) 326–48.

Boyd, Robert D., and J. Gordon Myers. "Transformative Education." *International Journal of Lifelong Learning* 7 (1988) 261–84.

Bray, Peter. "A Broader Framework for Exploring the Influence of Spiritual Experience in the Wake of Stressful Life Events." *Mental Health, Religion & Culture* 13 (2010) 293–308.

Bromiley, Geoffrey W. *The International Standard Bible Encyclopedia*. Vol. 4. Grand Rapids: Eerdmans, 1988.

Brookfield, Stephen D. *The Skillful Teacher*. San Francisco: Jossey-Bass, 1990.

———. "Transformative Learning as Ideology Critique." In *Learning as Transformation*, edited by Jack Mezirow et al., 125–50. San Francisco: Jossey-Bass, 2000.

Brown, Carolyn A. *"We Were All Slaves": African Miners, Culture, and Resistance at the Enugu Government Colliery*. Portsmouth, OH: Heinemann, 2003.

Brummett, Palmira J., et al. *Civilization Past and Present*. New York: Addison-Wesley, 2000.

Buber, Martin. *I and Thou*. New York: Scribner, 1970.

Byaruhanga, Christopher. *Bishop Alfred Robert Tucker and the Establishment of the Anglican Church in Uganda*. Nairobi: World Alive, 2007.

Calhoun, Lawrence, and Richard Tedeschi. "A Correlation Test of the Relationship between Post-Traumatic Growth, Religion, and Cognitive Processing." *Journal of Traumatic Stress* 13 (2000) 521–27.

———. "The Foundations of Posttraumatic Growth: New Considerations." *Psychological Inquiry* 15 (2004) 93–102.

———. *Handbook of Posttraumatic Growth: Research and Practice*. London: Erlbaum, 2006.

Cantor, Jeffrey. *Experiential Learning in Higher Education: Linking Classroom and Community*. Washington, DC: ASHE and the ERIC Clearinghouse on Higher Education, 1997.

Clark, Vicki L. Plano, and John W. Creswell. *The Mixed Methods Reader*. Thousand Oaks, CA: Sage, 2007.

Clarke, Adele. *Situational Analysis: Grounded Theory after the Postmodern Turn*. Thousand Oaks, CA: Sage, 2005.

Clarke, Clifton R. "In Our Mother Tongue: Vernacular Hermeneutics within African-Initiated Christianity in Ghana." *Trinity Journal of Church and Theology* 15 (2005) 52–68.

Cranton, Patricia. *Understanding and Promoting Transformative Learning: A Guide for Educators of Adults*. 2nd ed. San Francisco: Jossey-Bass, 2006.

Cranton, Patricia, and Merv Roy. "When the Bottom Falls Out of the Bucket: Toward a Holistic Perspective on Transformative Learning." *Journal of Transformative Education* 1 (2003) 6–98.

Dada, Adekunle. "Decolonizing Theological Education in Nigeria." *Doon Theological Journal* 6 (2009) 146–61.

Bibliography

Dana, Henry E., and Julius R. Mantey. *A Manual Grammar of the Greek New Testament.* Toronto: Macmillan, 1995.
Datta, Ansu, ed. *Education and Society: A Sociology of African Education.* London: Macmillan, 1984.
Delpit, Lisa. *Other People's Children's Cultural Conflicts in Classroom.* New York: New Press, 1995.
Dirkx, John M. "Engaging Emotions in Adult Learning: A Jungian Perspective on Emotion and Transformative Learning." *New Directions for Adult and Continuing Education* 109 (2006) 15–26.
Dubois, Jules, and Luc van den Wijngaert. *Initiation philosophique.* Kinshasa, DRC: Centre de Recherches Pédagogiques, 1997.
Duerr, Maia, et al. "Survey of Transformative and Spiritual Dimensions of Higher Education." *Journal of Transformative Education* 7 (2003) 177–211.
Elliot, Matthew A. *Faithful Feelings: Rethinking Emotion in the New Testament.* Grand Rapids: Kregel, 2006.
Estep, James R, Jr., et al. *A Theology for Christian Education.* Nashville: Academic, 2008.
Ethington, Corrina A., and Lee M. Wolfie. "Sex Differences in a Causal Model of Mathematics Achievement." *Journal for Research in Mathematics Education* 15 (1984) 361–77.
Etling, Arlen. "What Is Non-Formal Education?" *Journal of Agricultural Education* 34 (1993) 72–76.
Fafunwa, A. Babs, and J. U. Aisiku, eds. *Education in Africa: A Comparative Survey.* London: Allen & Unwin, 1982.
Fetherstone, Betts, and Rhys Kelly. "Conflict Resolution and Transformative Pedagogy: A Grounded Theory Research Project on Learning in Higher Education." *Journal of Transformative Education* 5 (2007) 262–85.
Flick, Uwe. *An Introduction to Qualitative Research.* 3rd ed. Thousand Oaks, CA: Sage, 2006.
Flicker, S., et al. "Ethical Dilemmas in Community Based Participatory Research: Recommendations for Institutional Review Boards." *Journal of Urban Health (New York Academy of Medicine)* 4 (2007) 478–93.
Foster, Richard J., and Kathryn A. Helmers. *Life with God: Reading the Bible for Spiritual Transformation.* New York: Harper, 2008.
Fowler, James. *Stages of Faith: The Psychology of Human Development and the Quest for Meaning.* San Francisco: Harper, 1981.
Freeman, Kimberly E., et al. "Do Learning Communities Enhance the Quality of Students' Learning and Motivation in STEM?" *Journal of Negro Education* 77 (2008) 227–40.
Freire, Paulo. *Pedagogy of the Oppressed.* New York: Seabury, 1970.
Freire, Paulo, and Antonio Faundez. *Learning to Question.* New York: Continuum, 1989.
Gall, Meredith D., et al. *Educational Research: An Introduction.* 6th ed. White Plains, NY: Longman, 1996.
Gaventa, Beverly R. *Acts of the Apostles.* Nashville: Abingdon, 2003.
Gillespie, Diane, and Molly Melching. "The Transformative Power of Democracy and Human Rights in Nonformal Education: The Case of Tostan." *Adult Education Quarterly* 60 (2010) 477–98.
Greene, Maxine. "Metaphor and Multiples: Representation, the Arts, and History." *Phi Delta Kappan* 78 (1997) 387–95.

Bibliography

Grof, Stanislav, and Christina Grof, eds. *Spiritual Emergency: When Personal Transformation Becomes a Crisis.* New York: Putnam, 1989.

———. *The Stormy Search for Self: A Guide to Personal Growth through Transformational Crises.* Los Angeles: Tarcher, 1990.

Gundry, Robert H. *Commentary on the New Testament: Verse-by-Verse Explanations with a Literal Translation.* Peabody, MA: Hendrickson, 2010.

Guthrie, Stan. "Rwanda: Unnatural Disaster." *Evangelical Missions Quarterly* 30 (1994) 444.

Habermas, Jurgen. *Knowledge and Human Interests.* Boston: Beacon, 1971.

Habermas, Ronald T. *Introduction to Christian Education and Formation: A Lifelong Plan for Christ-Centered Restoration.* Grand Rapids: Zondervan, 2008.

Healey, Joseph, and Donald Sybertz. *Towards an African Narrative Theology.* Nairobi: Paulines, 1996.

Hedin, Norma. "Experiential Learning: Theory and Challenges." *Christian Education Journal* 7 (2010) 107–17.

Heidegger, Martin. *Being and Time.* Translated by John Macquarrie and Edward Robinson. San Francisco: Harper, 1962.

Hollis, James. *The Eden Project: In Search of the Magical Order.* Toronto: Inner City, 1998.

Icenogle, Gareth Weldon. *Biblical Foundation for Small Groups Ministry: An Integrative Approach.* Westmont, IL: InterVarsity, 1994.

Imasogie, Osadolor. *Guidelines for Christian Theology in Africa.* Achimota, Ghana: Africa Christian Press, 1983.

Irvine, Jacqueline Jordan. "The Education of Children Whose Nightmares Come Both Day and Night." *Journal of Negro Education* 68 (1999) 244–54.

Jarvis, Peter. *Paradoxes of Learning: On Becoming an Individual in Society.* San Francisco: Jossey-Bass, 1992.

Jenkins, Philip. *The Next Christendom: The Coming of Global Christianity.* New York: Oxford University Press, 2002.

Kabeer, Naila. "Gender Equality and Women's Empowerment: A Critical Analysis of the Third Millennium Development Goal." *Gender and Development* 13 (2005) 13–24.

———. "Resources, Agency, Achievements: Reflections on the Measurements of Women's Empowerment." *Development and Change* 3 (1999) 463–82.

Kasyoka, John M. M. *An Introduction to Philosophy of Religion.* Eldoret, Kenya: Zapf Chancery, 2008.

Kazeem, Aramide, et al. "School Attendance in Nigeria: Understanding the Impact and Intersection of Gender, Urban-Rural Residence, and Socioeconomic Status." *Comparative Education Review* 54 (2010) 295–319.

Kelly, Gail Paradise. *French Colonial Education: Essays on Vietnam and West Africa.* New York: AMS, 2000.

Kenyatta, Jomo. *Facing Mount Kenya.* 2nd ed. Nairobi: Heinemann, 1984.

Kim, Jonathan. "Cognitive and Faith Formation: A Reflection on the Interrelationship of Schema, Thema and Faith." *Christian Education Journal* 4 (2004) 308–21.

King, Kathleen P. "Educational Technology That Transforms: Educator's Transformational Learning Experiences in Professional Development." In *Proceeding of the 41st Annual Adult Education Research Conference,* edited by Thomas J. Sork et al., 211–15. Vancouver: University of British Columbia Press, 2000.

———. "Examining Learning Activities and Transformational Learning." *International Journal of University Adult Education* 36 (1997) 23–37.

Bibliography

———. *Handbook of Evolving Research of Transformative Learning: Based on the Learning Activities Survey*. 10th anniversary ed. Charlotte, NC: Information Age, 2009.
Kingsbury, Charles Edward. "Barriers and Facilitators to Teaching for Critical Reflective Thought in Christian Higher Education in Anglophone Africa." PhD diss., Florida State University, 2002.
Kistemaker, Simon. *New Testament Commentary: Exposition of the Acts of the Apostles*. Grand Rapids: Baker Academic, 2002.
Kizito, Ahindukha, and B. A. Ondigi. "An Analysis of the Factors That Influence Teacher Attrition in Both Public and Private Secondary Schools in Kisumu City, Kenya." *Fountain Journal of Educational Research* 4 (2010) 90–103.
Kolb, David A. *Experiential Learning: Experience as the Source of Learning and Development*. Englewood Cliffs, NJ: Prentice-Hall, 1984.
Kombo, James Henry. *The Doctrine of God in African Christian Thought: The Holy Trinity, Theological Hermeneutics and the African Intellectual Culture*. Boston: Brill, 2007.
Kotter, John. *The Heart of Change: Real-Life Stories of How People Change Their Organizations*. Boston: Harvard Business School Press, 2002.
Kuhn, Thomas. *The Structure of Scientific Revolutions*. Chicago: University of Chicago Press, 1962.
Kwabena, Dei Ofori-Attah. "The British Curriculum Development in West Africa: A Historical Discourse." *Review of Education* 52 (2006) 409–23.
Lawrence, Terry Anne, et al. "Refocusing on the Learning in 'Integration of Faith and Learning.'" *Journal of Research on Christian Education* 14 (2005) 17–50.
Lewis, Linda H., and Carol J. Williams. "Experiential Learning: Past and Present." In *Experiential Learning: A New Approach*, edited by Lewis Jackson and Rosemary S. Caffarella, 5–16. San Francisco: Jossey-Bass, 1994.
Lewis, Suzanne Grant. *Education in Africa*. Philadelphia: Mason Crest, 2007.
Lingenfelter, Judith E., and Sherwood G. Lingenfelter. Sherwood. *Teaching Cross-Culturally: An Incarnational Model for Learning and Teaching*. Grand Rapids: Baker Academic, 2003.
Lombard, B. J. J., and M. M. Grosser. "Critical Thinking Abilities among Prospective Educators: Ideals versus Realities." *South African Journal of Education* 24 (2004) 212–16.
Manik, Sadhana. "To Greener Pastures: Transnational Teacher Migration from South Africa." *Perspectives in Education* 25 (2007) 55–65.
Marshall, I. Howard. *The Book of Acts: An Introduction and Commentary*. England: InterVarsity, 1980.
Marshall-Lucette, Sylvie, et al. "Developing Locally Based Research Capacity in Uganda." *International Nursing Review* 54 (2007) 227–33.
Martin, Arlene, and June Trueax. *Transformative Dimensions of Mentoring: Implications Practice in the Training of Early Childhood Teachers*. China-US Conference on Education. Collected Papers, July 9–13, 1997.
Matemba, Yonah Hisbon. "Religious Education in the Context of Sub-Sahara Africa: The Malawian Example." *British Journal of Religious Education* 31 (2000) 41–51.
McCracken, John. "Livingstonia in the Development of Malawi: A Reassessment." *Bulletin of the Scottish Institute of Missionary Studies* 10 (1994) 3–12.
Merriam, Sharan. "The Role of Cognitive Development in Mezirow's Transformative Learning Theory." *Adult Education Quarterly* 55 (2004) 60–68.

Bibliography

Merriam, Sharan B., and Gabo Ntseane. "Transformational Learning in Botswana: How Culture Shapes the Process." *Adult Education Quarterly* 58 (2008) 183–97.

Mezirow, Jack. "A Critical Theory of Adult Learning and Education." *Adult Education Quarterly* 32 (1981) 3–24.

———. *A Critical Theory of Self-Directed Learning*. San Francisco: Jossey-Bass, 1985.

———. *Education for Perspective Transformation: Women's Re-entry Programs in Community College*. New York: Teachers College, Columbia University, 1978.

———. "Perspective Transformation." *Adult Education Quarterly* 28 (1978) 100–110.

———. "Transformation Theory and Cultural Context: A Reply to Clark and Wilson." *Adult Education Quarterly* 41 (1991) 188–92.

———. *Transformative Dimensions of Adult Learning*. San Francisco: Jossey-Bass, 1991.

———. "Transformative Learning as Discourse." *Journal of Transformative Education* 5 (2003) 8–63.

———. "Understanding Transformation Theory." *Adult Education Quarterly* 44 (1994) 222–32.

Mezirow, Jack, Robert Kegan, et al. *Learning as Transformation: Critical Perspectives on a Theory in Progress*. San Francisco: Jossey-Bass, 2000.

Mezirow, Jack, Victoria J. Marsick, et al. *Fostering Critical Reflection in Adulthood: A Guide to Transformative and Emancipatory Learning*. San Francisco: Jossey-Bass, 1990.

Miheso, Marguerite K. "The Relationship between Interactive Teaching and the Acquisition of High Order Thinking Skills in Mathematics Classrooms: The Kenyan Experience." *African Journal of Education Studies* 1 (2005) 73–79.

Moulton, H. K. *A Concordance to the Greek Testament*. 5th ed. Edinburgh: T. & T. Clark, 1978. Originally published 1897, edited by W. F. Moulton and A. S. Geden.

Mungazi, Dickson A. *Colonial Education for Africans: George Stark's Policy in Zimbabwe*. New York: Praeger, 1991.

Murove, Munyaradzi Felix, ed. *African Ethics: An Anthology of Comparative and Applied Ethics*. Scottsville, South Africa: University of Kwazulu-Natal Press, 2009.

Murshida, Hassan, and Mehta K. Kalyani. "Grief Experience of Bereaved Malay/Muslim Youths in Singapore: The Spiritual Dimension." *International Journal of Children's Spirituality* 15 (2010) 45–57.

Musyoki, Rachel N. "Social Indicators: Levels and Trends in Sub-Saharan Africa." In *Realising African Development: A Millennial Analysis*, Purna C. Samanta and Raj Kumar Sen. Calcutta: Centre for Indo-African Development Studies, 2001.

Ntamushobora, Faustin. "An Exploration of Education for Holistic Transformation in Selected Christian and Public Universities in Kenya." PhD diss., Talbot School of Theology, 2012.

———. *From Trials to Triumphs: The Voice of Habakkuk to the Suffering African Christian*. Eugene, OR: Wipf & Stock, 2009.

———. "Toward an Understanding and Practice of Transformative Learning in Africa." *Common Ground Journal* 5 (2008) 69–80.

———. *Transformation through the Different Other: A Rendezvous of Giving and Receiving*. Eugene, OR: Wipf & Stock, 2013.

Ochieng, Digolo Patrick Obonyo. "Pedagogical Issues in Education in Kenya." *Fountain Journal of the School of Education* 3 (2009) 81–95.

Oladipo, Olusegun. Introduction to *The Third Way in African Philosophy: Essays in Honor of Kwasi Wiredu*, edited by Olesugun Oladipo. Ibadan, Nigeria: Hope, 2002.

Bibliography

Omotayo, Dare Michael, et al. "Management of Universal Basic Education Scheme (UBE) for Qualitative Education in Nigeria." *Education* 129 (2008) 308–15.

Opata, Damian U. *Essays on Igbo World View.* Nsukka: AP Express, 1998.

Orr, David W. "What Is Education For?" *Trumpeter* 8 (1991) 99–102.

Ouma, Gerald W., and Fredrick Q. Gravenir. "Globalization and the Need for Market Driven Programs: The Challenge for Public Higher Education in Kenya." *African Journal of Education Studies* 1 (2005) 9–18.

Percy, Rachel. "The Contribution of Transformative Learning Theory to the Practice of Participatory Research and Extension: Theoretical Reflections." *Agriculture and Human Values* 22 (2005) 127–36.

Peterson, David G. *The Acts of the Apostles.* Pillar New Testament Commentary. Grand Rapids: Eerdmans, 2009.

Robinson, Donald W. B. "Communion." In *The International Standard Bible Encyclopedia*, edited by Geoffrey W. Bromiley, 1:752–53. Grand Rapids: Eerdmans, 1979.

Saucy, Robert L. "The Heart: How Does Growth Take Place?" Working manuscript. Published as *Minding the Heart: The Way of Spiritual Transformation.* Grand Rapids: Kregel, 2013.

———. "Theology of Human Nature." Chapter 1 in *Christian Perspectives on Being Human: A Multidisciplinary Approach to Integration*, edited by James P. Moreland and David M. Ciocchi. Grand Rapids: Baker, 1993.

Selzer, Elizabeth. "Effectiveness of a Seminary's Training and Mentoring Program and Subsequent Job Satisfaction of Its Graduates." *Journal of Research on Christian Education* 17 (2008) 25–53.

Sethi, Meera. "Return and Reintegration of Qualified African Nationals." In *Brain Drain and Capacity Building in Africa*, edited by J. M. Sibry Tapsoba et al., 38–48. Addis Ababa: UN Economic Commission for Africa, 2000.

Setiloane, Gabriel Molehe. *African Theology: An Introduction.* Johannesburg: Skotaville, 1986.

Sheldrake, Philip. "What Is Spirituality?" Chapter 1 in *Exploring Christian Spirituality*, edited by K. Collins. Grand Rapids: Baker, 2000.

Sifuna, Daniel Namusonge. *Development of Education in Africa: The Kenyan Experience.* Nairobi: Initiatives, 1990.

Sipos, Yona. "Achieving Transformative Sustainability Learning: Engaging Head, Hands and Heart." *International Journal of Sustainability in Higher Education* 9 (2006) 68–86.

Smallbones, Jackie L. "Teaching Bible for Transformation." *Christian Education Journal* 4 (2007) 293–307.

Spencer, A. R. "Fellowship." In *Mercer Dictionary of the Bible*, edited by Watson E. Mills Natson, 298–99. Macon, GA: Mercer University Press, 1991.

Spivak, Gayatri Chakravorty. *A Critique of Postcolonial Reason: Toward a History of the Vanishing Present.* Cambridge: Harvard University Press, 1999.

Starcher, Richard L. "A Non-western Doctoral Program in Theology for Africans in Africa." *Christian Higher Education* 3 (2004) 295–311.

Stern, P. N., and C. J. Porr. *Essentials of Accessible Grounded Theory.* Walnut Creek, CA: Left Coast, 2011.

Strauss, Anselm L., and Juliet Corbin. *Basics of Qualitative Research.* 2nd ed. London: Sage, 1998.

Bibliography

Strauss, Mark L. *The Davidic Messiah in Luke-Acts*. Sheffield, UK: Sheffield Academic, 1995.

Striano, Maura. "Managing Educational Transformation in the Globalized World: A Deweyan Perspective." *Educational Theory* 59 (2004) 379–93.

Szirmai, Adam. *The Dynamic of Socio-Economic Development: An Introduction*. Cambridge: Cambridge University Press, 2005.

Taylor, Edward W., ed. "Analyzing Research on Transformative Learning Theory." In *Learning as Transformation*, edited by J. Mezirow et al., 285–328. San Francisco: Jossey-Bass, 2000.

———. *Teaching for Change: Fostering Transformative Learning in the Classroom*. San Francisco: Jossey-Bass, 2006.

———. "Transformative Learning Theory." *New Directions for Adult and Continuing Education* 119 (2008) 5–15.

———. "An Update on Transformative Learning Theory: A Critical Review of the Empirical Research (1999–2005)." *International Journal of Lifelong Education* 26 (2007) 173–91.

Taylor, W. H. "Missionary Education in Africa Reconsidered: The Presbyterian Education Impact in Eastern Nigeria, 1846–1974." *African Affairs* 83 (1984) 189–205.

Tedeschi, Richard G., et al., eds. *Posttraumatic Growth: Positive Changes in the Aftermath of Crisis*. Mahwah, NJ: Erlbaum, 1998.

Teferra, Damtew, and Philip Altbach. "African Higher Education: Challenges for the 21st Century." *Higher Education* 47 (2004) 21–50.

Timms, David. *Living the Lord's Prayer*. Minneapolis: Bethany House, 2008.

Tolliver, Derise E., and Elizabeth J. Tisdell. "Engaging Spirituality in the Transformative Higher Education Classroom." *New Direction for Adult Continuing Education* 109 (2006) 37–47.

Unger, Merrill F. *The New Unger's Bible Dictionary*. Chicago: Moody, 1988.

Usher, Robin, and Nicky Solomon. "Experiential Learning and the Shaping of Subjectivity in the Work-Place." *Studies in the Education of Adults* 31 (1999) 155–63.

Van der Merwe, Marietjie, and Ruth M. Albertyn. "Transformation through Training: Application of Emancipatory Methods in a Housing Education Programme for Rural Women in South Africa." *Community Development Journal* 45 (2010) 149–68.

Van de Walle, Nicolas. *African Economies and the Politics of Permanent Crisis, 1979–1999*. Cambridge: Cambridge University Press, 2001.

Van der Walt, Barend Johannes. "The Challenge of Christian Higher Education on the African Continent in the Twenty-First Century." *Christian Higher Education* 1 (2002) 195–227.

Verderber, Rudolph F. *Communicate!* Belmont, CA: Wadsworth, 1985.

Wamukuru, D. K., et al. "The Challenge of Implementing Free Primary Education in Kenya and Its Effect on Teacher Effectiveness: The Teacher Perspective." *African Journal of Education Studies* 1 (2005) 1–16.

Ward, Kevin. "Christianity, Colonialism and Missions." In *Cambridge History of Christianity*, edited by Hugh McLeod, 71–88. Cambridge: Cambridge University Press, 2006.

Webber, Sheila Simsarian. "Development of Cognitive and Affective Trust in Teams." *Small Group Research* 39 (2008) 746–69.

Bibliography

Wighting, Mervyn, and Liu Jing. "Relationships between Sense of School Community and Sense of Religious Commitment among Christian High School Students." *Journal of Research on Christian Education* 18 (2009) 56–68.

Witherington, Ben, III. *The Acts of the Apostles: A Socio-Rhetorical Commentary*. Grand Rapids: Eerdmans, 1998.

Wolhuter, C. C., and H. J. Steyn. "Learning from South-South Comparison: The Education Systems of South Africa and Madagascar." *South African Journal of Education* 23 (2003) 29–35.

Woods, Peter. *Successful Writing for Qualitative Research*. 2nd ed. London: Routledge, 2006.

Wright, Christopher. *Salvation Belongs to God: Celebrating the Bible's Story*. Downers Grove: InterVarsity, 2007.

Yount, William R. *Created to Learn: A Christian Teacher's Introduction to Educational Psychology*. Nashville: Broadman & Holman, 1996.

———. "Experiential Learning." In *Evangelical Dictionary of Christian Education*, edited by M. Anthony, 276–77. Grand Rapids: Baker, 2001.

Zeleza, Paul Tiyambe, and Adebayo O. Olukoshi, eds. *African Universities in the Twenty-First Century*. Dakar: CODESRIA, 2004.

Zhao, Chun-Mei, and G. D. Kuh. "Adding Value: Learning Communities and Student Engagement." *Research in Higher Education* 28 (2004) 503–25.

Index

Note: A "t" following the page number indicates a table. All Scripture references are gathered under the heading "Scripture references."

6-3-3-4 educational system (Nigeria), 25–26

Abidogun, Jamaine, 13, 19–20
academics, 28–29, 32. *See also* teachers
academic success, 52–53
action research, 68
actions, change of, 82
active learning strategies, 62–63
Adam, 83
Addis Ababa University (Ethiopia), 28
Adekunle, O. Dada, 22–23
Adeyemi, Michael B., 10, 12
Adeyemo, Tokunboh, 6, 17
Adeyinka, Augustus A., 10, 12
Adkins-Coleman, Theresa A., 46–47
adult education, 3, 36–37, 66
affective/relational dimension of transformative learning, 48–56, 64, 105, 106, 117. *See also* emotions; relationships
affective trust, 50–52, 96
Africa
  economy of, 6–7, 25–28
  forms of spirituality in, 14
  history of education in, 10–32, 63
  holistic transformation in Kenya, 97–118
  natural resources of and poverty in, 6–7, 63
  need for holistic education in, 1–9
  See also education
Africa International University (AIU)
  description of, 120
  permission to do research, 126
  See also study of holistic transformation in Kenya
African American students
  effectiveness of learning communities, 45–46, 54–56
  themes of successfully facilitated engagement with, 46–47
African pedagogical methods, 2–4
African political leaders, 17
African Renaissance, 29
African sword, 89–90
African thought, 91
African worldview, 2–3, 4, 18, 39–40, 111, 114
ahantu (place and time), 91
Aisiku, J. U., 10
Akilagpa, Sawyerr, 1–2, 25
Albertyn, Ruth M., 38, 63–64, 65, 69
Allah, 60–61
Alliance High School (Kenya), 17
Alston, Sharon T., 45–46
Altbach, Philip, 28

143

Index

ambivalence to education, 13
analysis, 43
Ansell, Nicola, 23-24
apodechomai (accept with satisfaction), 82
application, 43
apprenticeship, 12, 19, 24
authenticity
  as beginning of transformation, 81
  development of, 49-50, 60
  as goal of transformation, 68, 69, 70, 102
  spiritual development of, 57
  of teachers, 49
  See also identity
autobiographical techniques, 39
axial categories, 99
axial coding, 100

Balk, D. E., 58, 92
banking method of learning, 7-8, 34-35. *See also* formal education by colonizers; postcolonial African education
Bantu thinking, 91
baptism, 82-83
Barkan, Joel D., 30-31
Bassey, Magnus O., 16, 17
Baur, John, 17
behavioral expectations, 47
behavioral transformation, 106
believers. *See* Christians
Bennetts, Christine, 66, 69, 105
bereavement, 58-61
Bible
  fruits of application to life, 106
  as transforming truth, 73-75, 84-86, 95, 111
  See also Scripture references
Biblical view of holistic transformation, 71-96, 105-7
Biola University, 98
Bloom's taxonomy of cognitive domain, 42-43, 48
Bock, Darrell L., 78, 79, 80, 81
Botswana, 28, 39-40, 70
Boyd, Robert D., 45
boys, 20-21

brain drain, 25, 28-29, 32
brainstorming, 65
Bray, Peter, 58, 92
British educational system in Africa, 7, 14-15
Bromiley, Geoffrey W., 77
Brookfield, Stephen D., 49
Buber, Martin, 49-50
Burton, Larry D., 62-63

Calhoun, Lawrence, 58, 59
Calvinia, South Africa, 65
case studies, 63, 65
CBPR (Community-Based Participatory Research), 68
Character Contracts of TM Program, 54
Christ-centered worldview, 8
Christian higher education in East Africa, 5
Christianity. *See* church
Christians
  attraction of unbelievers, 93
  fellowship of, 87-92, 95
  genocide in Rwanda and, 6
  holistic transformation of, 6, 94-95
  journey of, 83
  prayer life of, 86-87, 95
  salvation of, 81-82, 83-84
  sanctification of, 84-92
  study of Word of God, 84-86, 95
  in Sub-Saharan Africa, 9
  See also church; study of holistic transformation in Kenya
Christian universities
  description of, 120-21
  letter to and responses from sampled universities, 124-27
Christian university graduates
  community service, 110, 112-13
  comparison of public university graduates to, 107
  profiles of, 130t
  See also CHRUN1-12; study of holistic transformation in Kenya
CHRUN1, 103, 130t
CHRUN2, 101, 102, 130t
CHRUN3, 101, 130t

Index

CHRUN4, 103, 130t
CHRUN5, 130t
CHRUN6, 111, 130t
CHRUN7, 130t
CHRUN8, 108, 130t
CHRUN9, 130t
CHRUN10, 108, 130t
CHRUN11, 103, 108, 130t
CHRUN12, 110, 130t
church
   Africans' view of, 8
   challenges in Africa, 5–6, 18
   effect on dual sex political system, 20
   in Nigeria, 22
   recommendations for, 115
   school attendance and, 21
   as venue for community transformation, 8, 110, 112–13, 114
   See also Christians; missionaries; theological education (Nigeria)
civilizing mission, 14–15
Clarke, Clifton R., 23
cognitive domain, taxonomy of, 42–43
cognitive task, 47
cognitive trust, 50–52, 96
collaborative learning, 39, 52–56, 68
collaborative pedagogy of learning communities, 45–46
colonialism, 14
colonial period. See formal education by colonizers
communalism, 12, 13, 102, 105–6
communication
   acquisition and validation of personal meanings, 38
   Habermas on, 36
   role in transformative learning, 47
community, 51–52, 63
Community-Based Participatory Research (CBPR), 68
community relationships
   effect on processing and interpretation of events, 39–40
   importance to Africans, 40
   religious commitment related to, 52
   transformation through, 95
community responsibility, 39–40, 95
community service
   educational preparation for, 8
   of study participants, 105, 107, 110, 112–13
   Tostan's curriculum encouraging, 3
community transformation
   as aspect of transformation learning, 39, 65–66
   church as venue for, 8, 110, 112–13, 114
   educational system fostering, 6, 8, 63–67, 69, 110
   as fruit of salvation, 83–84
   as goal of education, 10
   as goal of Tostan, 3
   work of study graduates, 105
   See also social/community transformation
Competency Contracts of TM Program, 54
comprehension, 43
concepts, 99
confessional sharing, 90
conflict transformation, 43–45
conscientization, 34, 35
consciousness, 35
consciousness-raising, 64–65
contemplative practices, 39
content reflection, 41, 101
context
   effects of teaching within, 34
   formal education in Africa unrelated to, 5, 7, 22
   need for incorporation in education, 4, 10, 102–3, 107, 110, 118
   in postcolonial African education, 22
   role in transformative learning, 8, 9, 10, 33, 39, 103
   as standard of judgment of educational effectiveness, 10
   traditional African education related to, 2–3, 11
cooperative learning strategies, 62–63
Corbin, Juliet, 78
Cranton, Patricia, 49, 50–52, 57
creative expression, 39
creative thinking skills, 4, 24
critical discourse, 35, 48
critical incident analysis, 65

Index

critical reflection
 aspects of, 41–42
 basis for Mezirow's concept of, 35, 48
 as core of transformative learning, 68
 defined, 40–41
 lacking in post-colonial education, 30
 lacking in traditional African education, 12
 outcome of, 33
 requirements for, 5, 40–41
 taxonomy of, 42–43
 in transformative learning, 40–47
critical self-reflection, 40–41
critical self-reflection of assumption, 42
 basis for Mezirow's concept of, 35, 48, 102
 as central element of perspective transformation, 37
 forms of, 42
critical theory of adult learning, 36
critical thinking skills
 formal education by colonizers lacking, 1, 7–8, 15, 32
 as necessity for educational contribution to society, 1
 need for in Africa, 4, 7–8
 outcome of, 33, 64–65
 postcolonial education lacking, 24
 teacher training lacking, 29–31
 of Western formal education, 102
critical transitivity, 35
culture
 connection to spirituality, 57
 education related to, 3, 14–15, 19, 39–40
 See also context; relevance
curriculum
 of Christian vs. public universities, 107
 in East Africa, 5
 of formal colonial education, 14–16
 in postcolonial Africa, 16, 22–23
 for teacher education, 28
 of Tostan organization, 3
 of traditional African education, 11, 16–17
 for transformative learning, 4, 56–57

 See also context; relevance
"cut to the heart," 80

Dana, D., 38
Dana, Henry E., 81
Datta, Ansu, 30–31
David (king of Israel), 78
democracy in the classroom, 1–2, 11, 35
dialogic learning, 36–37, 64–65
dictators, 17
Dirkx, John M., 8
disciples. See Christians
disorientation dilemma
 basis for Mezirow's concept of, 35, 48
 confirmation of Mezirow's concept, 102
 critical reflection initiated by, 68
 reflection following, 41
 spiritual transformation through, 58–62, 92, 95, 104–5, 106
 triggers for, 39, 48, 49
distorted assumptions
 critical evaluation of, 65–66, 69, 95, 102
 types of, 38, 64
doctors, 28
domains of learning, 34, 36–37
Duerr, Maia, 38

early trust, 50–51
East Africa, 5, 30–31
economic challenges, 25–28, 32
economic empowerment, 66–67
economic responsibilities, 11
economy, 6–7, 25–28
education
 Biblical and theological view of, 71–96
 curriculum for holistic transformation in Africa, 4, 56–57
 economic challenges, 25–28
 goal of, 10
 integration of spiritual dimension, 62–63
 in Kenya, 69–70
 as means of fighting poverty, 6, 7
 need for holistic education in Africa, 1–9

Index

non-formal education, 2-4
  in postcolonial Africa, 18-31
  professional challenges, 28-31
  recommendations for practices in Africa, 114-16
  requirements for contribution to society, 1-2, 4, 5
  rooted in African values and worldview, 2-3
  school attendance, 3-4, 20-21, 24, 31-32
  socio-cultural challenges, 18-21
  study of in Kenya, 97-118
  theory of education for holistic transformation, 33-70
  of women, 3-4, 20-21
  See also context; curriculum; formal education by colonizers; pedagogical methods; relevance; traditional education in Africa
Elliot, Matthew A., 80
emancipator teaching methods, 64-65
emancipatory learning, 36
emotion-focused coping, 60, 61
emotions
  awakening by changed thoughts, 79-82
  bereavement, 58-61
  effect on cognitive process, 80
  leading to change of will and actions, 82, 96, 105, 106
  role in transformative learning, 44-45
  See also affective/relational dimension of transformative learning
empathy, 47
employment
  of girls, 23-25, 31-32
  of teachers and academics, 26-31
empowerment
  defined, 63, 110
  as goal of Tostan, 3
  learning and development through, 44
  levels of, 63-64
  methods of, 64-65, 69
epistemic critical self-reflection on assumptions, 42

epistemic meaning perspective, 38
epistemological distorted assumptions, 64, 65
eternal life, 83
ethical teaching, 12
Ethiopia, 28
ethnocentrism, 71-72
Etling, Arlen, 67
eureka, 72-73, 108, 111, 112-13, 117
evaluation, 43
experiences, 72, 73-75
experiential learning, 67-68
experiential pedagogy, 39
extrinsic motivation, 45

Fafunwa, A. Babs, 10, 16
faith, 58-63, 81-82, 95
family, 20, 59-60
Faundez, Antonio, 35
fellowship, 87-92, 95
Fetherstone, Betts, 33, 43-45, 96
financial problems. See economic challenges
Flick, Uwe, 99, 100
folktales, 12
formal education by colonizers
  British and French curriculum for, 14-16
  consequences of, 14-15, 17, 19, 22
  effectiveness of, 1, 3-4, 7-8, 13, 14-20, 63
  goals of, 5, 7, 14, 15, 16, 17
  methodology of, 1, 5, 7, 14, 15, 18, 20, 32, 103
formal experiential learning, 67
Foster, Richard, 85-86
Fowler, James, 57, 58
FPE (Free Primary Education), 27
frames of reference, 43, 48
framework of psycho-spiritual transformation, 58-62
freedom, 72
Freeman, Kimberly E., 45-46
Free Primary Education (FPE), 27
Freire, Paulo, 7-8, 34-35, 64
French colonial education in Africa, 15-16
Friberg, Barbara, 72

Index

friends, 59–60
fulfillment, 105
functionalism, 12

Gambia, 14–15
Gaventa, Beverly R., 80
gender roles, 19–20, 39–40
"getting it"/challenge stage of learning, 44
Ghana
    colonial education in, 14–15
    emigration of doctors and academics from, 28
    methodology of higher education, 30–31
    Trinity College, Achemota, 17
Gillespie, Diane, 3
girls
    education and employment of, 23–25, 31–32
    education of, 2, 3, 30
    loss of indigenous skills, 19–20
    school attendance, 20–21
globalization, 1, 5, 8, 13
God the Father
    African view of, 22
    as refiner of souls, 92–93
    reflection on, 61
    relationship with Holy Spirit, 88
    relationship with Jesus, 79, 88
    restoration of relationship with, 83
    sanctification of believers, 84–92
    as theme of Kenya study, 110–11
    as transformer, 94, 106, 109
Gravenir, Fredrick Q., 5
Great Other. *See* God the Father; Holy Spirit
grief. *See* bereavement
Groenewald, Cornie J., 63–64
Grof, Christina, 58–59, 60, 92
Grof, Stansilav, 58–59, 60, 92
Grosser, M. M., 29
group communication levels, 90
Gundry, Robert H., 82

Habermas, Ronald T., 34, 36, 88
habits of mind, transforming, 43
heart of man, 91

Hedin, Norma, 67
Heidegger, Martin, 50
holistic transformation
    in Acts 2, 94–95
    Biblical and theological view of, 71–96
    critical reflection in transformative learning, 40–47
    curriculum for, 4, 56–57
    defined, 33, 100
    findings from research in Kenya, 97–118
    methods of, 75, 76–96
    need for education for in Africa, 1–4
    Peter's sermon on day of Pentecost, 70, 75, 76–82
    rationale for study of education for, 4–9
    salvation as, 83–84
    theory of education for, 33–70
    See also education for holistic transformation; study of holistic transformation in Kenya; transformative learning
Hollis, James, 50
Holy Spirit
    as agent of transformation, 81, 96, 106, 109, 111, 117
    coming of, 75–76
    relationship with God the Father and Jesus, 88
    sanctification of believers, 84

Icenogle, Gareth Weldon, 90
identity
    contextualization of curriculum and, 103
    loss of through colonial education, 13, 14, 15, 19–20, 31
    spiritual development of, 57, 60
    See also authenticity
IFL (integration of faith and learning), 62–63
Iheberere, Chioma, 25–26
ikintu (objects), 91
Imasogie, Osadolor, 22
indigenous education. *See* traditional education in Africa

Index

indigenous gender roles, 19, 20
indigenous knowledge, 19–20
informal experiential learning, 67
inner reflection, 71, 72
instrumental learning, 36–37
integration of faith and learning (IFL), 62–63
intellectual transformation, 105, 107–9
intercession, 86
interface/interpersonal empowerment, 63–64
internal mobility, 28
internships, 67–68, 107
inter-personal commitment, 52
interpersonal empowerment, 63–64
interview participants' profiles, 130–31t
intransitive thought, 35
intrinsic motivation, 45–46
Introduction to Conflict Resolution (college course), 43–45
Irvine, Jacqueline Jordan, 47
Islam. *See* Muslims

Jarvis, Peter, 49
Jensen, Leif, 20
Jesus Christ
    as Messiah, 78–79
    miracles of, 78
    prediction of coming of Holy Spirit, 77
    redemptive act of, 88
    relationship with God the Father, 79, 88
    relationship with Holy Spirit, 88
    salvation through faith in, 83
    transformative ministry of, 93
    use of provoking thoughts, 74
Jing, Liu, 52
John the Baptist, 77
Josephus, 78

Kabeer, Naila, 63
Kagame, Alex, 91
Kalyani, Mehta K., 60
Kamau, C. W., 27
Kapp, Chris A., 63–64
Kasyoka, John M. M., 91
katanyssomai (cause sharp pain), 80

katenygēsantēnkardian (cut to the heart), 81
Kazeem, Aramide, 20
Kelly, Gail Paradise, 15
Kelly, Rhys, 33, 43–45, 96
Kenya
    Alliance High School, 17
    education in, 69–70
    Free Primary Education and Universal Primary Education in, 27
    Kikuyu system in, 18
    study of education, 69–71, 97–118
    study of teacher attrition, 26
    teacher shortages, 26–27
    transformative learning theory in, 8–9
Kenya Certificate of Secondary Education (KCSE), 30
Kenyatta, Jomo, 18
Kikuyu system (Kenya), 18
Kingsbury, Charles Edward, 5, 30
King's College Budo (Uganda), 17
Kistemaker, Simon, 76
Kisumu City, Kenya, 26
Kizito, Ahindukha, 26
knowledge, 43
koinōneō (to share), 88
koinōnia (union with others), 87–92
Kolb, David A., 64
Kotter, John, 55
Kuh, G. D., 52–53
Kuhn, Thomas, 34
Kwabena, Dei Ofori-Attah, 7, 14–15

Ladson-Billings, Gloria, 46
language of instruction
    of formal colonial education, 14, 15, 31
    in Kenya, 69
    in mission schools, 14
    for theological education, 23
    Tostan, 3
    use of vernacular suggested, 23
Lawrence, Terry Anne, 62–63
learning
    active learning strategies, 62–63

Index

banking method, 7–8, 34–35. *See also* formal education by colonizers; postcolonial African education
collaborative, 39, 52–56, 68
cooperative learning strategies, 62–63
critical theory of adult learning, 36
dialogic, 36–37, 64–65
domains of, 34, 36–37
emancipatory, 36
experiential, 67–68
instrumental, 36–37
participatory, 64–65
practical, 36
processes of, 37
self-directed, 36–37, 66
self-reflective, 36–37, 37, 64–65, 72, 102, 104–5, 117
service, 39
stages of, 44
technical, 36
ways of, 43–46
See also transformative learning
learning communities
academic success related to, 52–56
effectiveness for African American students, 45–46
religious commitment related to, 52
transformation promoted by, 63
lectio divina (spiritual reading), 85
Lesotho, 23–24
Lewis, Linda H., 67
Lewis, Suzanne Grant, 10, 13
life-crisis triggers
critical reflection initiated by, 68
Mezirow's theory and, 35, 48
spiritual transformation through, 58–62, 92, 95, 106
types of, 39, 48, 49
life expectancy, 7
Life with God: Reading the Bible for Spiritual Transformation (Foster), 85–86
Lingenfelter, Judith E., 103
Lingenfelter, Sherwood G., 103
literature review for holistic transformation

affective/relational dimension of transformative learning, 48–56
critical reflection in transformative learning, 40–47
origin and development of transformative learning, 34–40
social/community transformation, 63–67
spiritual transformation, 56–63
study findings compared to, 100–101t, 117
Livingstonia Mission, Malawi, 16
Lomax, Ms. (teacher), 47
Lombard, B. J. J., 29

macro/socio-political empowerment, 63–64
Madagascar, 23
Maduewesi, B. U., 25–26
Malawi, 16
male labor migration, 24
Manik, Sadhana, 28–29
Mantey, Julius R., 81
marriage, 20
Marshall, I. Howard, 77
Martin, Arlene, 56
maternal education, effect on school attendance, 21
meaning, 38
meaning perspective
defined, 37
elaboration on, 43
transformation of, 41, 48, 102
types of, 38
meaning schemes, 37, 41, 48, 101
meaning transformation, 37
Melching, Molly, 3
mentoring, 19, 55–56, 95, 107
Mentoring Relationship of TM Program, 54, 55
Merriam, Sharan B., 39, 40–41
metanoēsate (repent), 81
metaphorical analysis, 65
metaphysical world, 39–40
methodology, 97–100. *See also* pedagogical methods
Mezirow, Jack
aspects of critical reflection, 41–42

Index

confirmation of theory of, 100–102
on distorted assumptions, 64
emphasis on critical reflection, 40
influences on theory of holistic transformation, 34–36
outline of derivative concept of adult education and development, 36–37
study of women returning to community college, 34
taxonomy of critical reflection, 42–43
theory of education for holistic transformation, 33, 48, 56, 66, 113, 117
on types of reflection, 41
on ways of learning, 43
micro/personal empowerment, 63
migration of teachers, 25, 28, 32
Miheso, Marguerite K., 29–30
Miller, Neva, 72
missionaries, 13, 14–15, 17
modeling, 52, 55
modernization, 14–15
Moi University (MU)
description of, 119
permission to do research, 128
See also study of holistic transformation in Kenya
Morrison, Ms. (teacher), 46–47
motivation, 45, 52
Mungazi, Dickson A., 5, 7
Murshida, Hassan, 60
Muslims, 21, 60–61
mutual encouragement, 52
Myers, J. Gordon, 45

Nairobi International School of Theology (NIST)
description of, 120–21
permission to do research, 127
See also study of holistic transformation in Kenya
narrative critical self-reflection of assumptions, 42
natural resources, 6, 9, 63
negotiating new relationships, 37
new realization, 72, 108
Nigeria

6—3-3—4 educational system in, 25–26
ambivalence to education in, 13
colonial education in, 14–15
gender gap in school attendance, 20–21
Nsukka secondary schools in, 19–20
theological education in, 22–23
Universal Basic Education in, 25–26
non-formal education, 2–4
non-formal experiential learning, 67
Northern Igbo people, 13, 19–20
"not getting it" stage of learning, 44
Nsukka secondary schools (Nigeria), 19–20
Ntseane, Gabo, 39
ntu metaphysics, 91
NVivo (version 9) program, 99
Nwosu, Constance C., 62–63

objective reframing, 42, 43
Obote, Milton, 17
Ochieng, Digolo Patrick Onbonyo, 5
Ochola, W. O., 27
Oladipo, Olusegun, 22–23
older relatives, 11, 18
Olukoshi, Adebayo O., 4
Omotayo, Dare Michael, 25–26
Ondigi, B. A., 26
openness, 1–2, 57
oral literature, 12
Orr, David W., 4
O'Sullivan (professor of transformative learning), 38
"the other"
African vs. Western concept of, 105–6
as theme of Kenya study, 110–11
transformation through, 111–12, 114, 117
Ouma, Gerald W., 5

paradigms, 34
parents, 2–3, 11
participatory learning, 64–65
participatory research, 68
paternal education, 21
Paul, Saint, 86

Index

pedagogical methods
    for African American students, 45–47
    experiential learning, 67–68
    of formal education by colonizers, 1, 5, 7, 14, 15, 18, 32, 103
    of Peter, 70, 75, 76–82
    of postcolonial African education, 23–24, 29, 30–31, 32
    of Tostan organization, 3–4
    of traditional education in Africa, 2–3, 11–12, 13, 18
    for transformative learning, 39, 43–46, 64–65, 103
peer relationships, 18, 44
Pentecost, 75–76, 79
Percy, Rachel, 64
perennialism, 12
personal empowerment, 63
personal meanings, 38
perspective transformation
    central concepts and element of, 37–38
    crisis as catalyst for, 48
    description of, 36
    frame of references resulting from, 48
    of graduate students, 108–9
    Peter's sermon on day of Pentecost as, 76–77
    process of, 48, 77, 117
    result of, 37
    spiritual reframing and, 62
    support of, 66
Peter, Saint
    incorrect assumptions of, 78–79
    sermon on day of Pentecost, 70, 75, 76–82
Peterson, David G., 76, 77, 78, 80, 85, 86, 89
poiēsomen (to do, perform, practice), 80
points of view, transforming, 43
postcolonial African education
    challenge of relevance of education, 22–25, 31
    consequences of, 22
    curriculum of, 16, 22–23
    economic challenges, 25–28, 31
    language of education, 31
    methodology, 23–24, 29, 30–31, 32
    professional challenges, 28–31
    socio-cultural challenges, 18–21, 31
post traumatic growth model, 58–62
poverty, 6–7, 9, 63
practical learning, 36
practice, implication for in Kenya study for, 114
praxis-knowledge, 80
prayer, 86–87, 95
premise reflection, 41, 101, 102
preparationism, 12
problem-focused coping, 60, 61
process reflection, 41–42, 101
professional challenges, 28–31
professional helpers, 59–60
promotive interaction, 44
protestant high schools, 17
psychological distorted assumptions, 64, 65
psychological intuition, 40
psychological meaning perspective, 38
psycho-spiritual transformation, 58–59
public school curriculum, 22
public universities
    description of, 119–20
    letter to and responses from sampled universities, 124–25, 128–29
public university graduates
    community service, 110, 112–13
    comparison of Christian university graduates to, 107
    profiles of, 130–31t
    See also PUBUN1–11; study of holistic transformation in Kenya
PUBUN1, 110, 130t
PUBUN2, 131t
PUBUN3, 104, 131t
PUBUN4, 131t
PUBUN5, 105, 131t
PUBUN6, 131t
PUBUN7, 109, 131t
PUBUN8, 102, 131t
PUBUN9, 131t
PUBUN10, 131t
PUBUN11, 131t

rationale for this study, 4–9

Index

recommendations for educational practice in Africa, 114–16
recommendations for further research, 116–17
reflection
   as key to transformation, 43–44
   types of, 41
   See also critical reflection; critical self-reflection; critical self-reflection of assumption
reflective diaries, 44
relational dimension of transformative learning, 48–56, 105. See also relationships
relationship renegotiation, 37
relationships
   acquisition and validation of personal meanings, 38
   authenticity and, 49–50
   development in Christian fellowship, 90–92
   development of trust in, 50–52
   effect on processing and interpretation of events, 39–40
   formal education by colonizers and, 18
   between God and believers, 86–87
   renegotiation and negotiating new ones, 37
   role in transformative learning, 35, 45–56, 68–69, 70, 102, 105, 117
   traditional education in Africa and, 18
relevance
   as challenge for postcolonial education in Africa, 22–25, 31
   of church teachings, 6
   of curriculum in East Africa, 5
   of formal colonial education, 16
   need for in African education, 10, 102, 107, 110, 118
   of Tostan, 3
   of traditional education in Africa, 11
religion, 22, 57. See also Christians; church; missionaries; Muslims; spirituality
religious commitment, 52
religious education
   in colonial Africa, 14–15
   in Nigeria, 22–23
   in traditional Africa, 11
   See also Peter, Saint; study of holistic transformation in Kenya
renegotiating relationships, 37
repentance, 77, 81–82
research
   implication for in Kenya study for, 113–14
   recommendation for further studies, 116–17
research questions, 97–98, 107–10, 122–23
respect, 46, 47
role-playing, 65
Roy, Merv, 50–52
Rwanda, genocide in, 6

sōzomenous (those being saved), 83
salvation
   as agent of transformation, 96
   of Jews at Pentecost, 81–82, 94
   sanctification and, 83–92
   work of emotions in, 106
sanctification, 84–92
Saucy, Robert L., 84, 86–87, 91, 92, 106
school attendance, 3–4, 20–21, 24, 31–32
school community, 52, 52–56
Scripture references
   Genesis 27:38, 80
   Genesis 34:7, 80
   Exodus 23:16, 75
   Leviticus 10:3, 80
   Leviticus 23:15–16, 75
   Numbers 11:29, 75
   Deuteronomy 16:9–12, 75
   Psalms 30:5, 93
   Proverbs 27:17, 89
   Isaiah 5:24, 76
   Isaiah 44:3, 75
   Ezekiel 36:27, 75
   Joel, 77
   Matthew 3:8, 82
   Matthew 5:3–4, 82
   Matthew 16:21, 78
   Matthew 18:8–9, 83

153

Index

Mark 2:1–13, 74
Luke 11:15, 78
Luke 18:18–30, 83
Luke 24:26, 78
John 3:1–12, 88
John 8:32, 72
John 14:26, 109
John 17:11, 88
John 17:17, 84
Acts 2, 70, 76–82, 89, 94–96, 106
Acts 2:2–4, 75
Acts 2:6, 76
Acts 2:11, 76
Acts 2: 12–13, 76
Acts 2:13, 81
Acts 2:15–35, 77–79
Acts 2:25–30, 78
Acts 2:32–36, 79
Acts 2:37, 77, 80–81
Acts 2:38, 81
Acts 2:41, 77, 82
Acts 2:42, 84, 86
Acts 2:42–47, 89
Acts 2:44–45, 88
Acts 2:46, 84
Acts 2:47, 83, 86, 93
Acts 3:1, 86
Acts 6:1–2, 89
Acts 6:7, 92
Acts 9:6, 82
Acts 10:37–38, 78
Acts 16:5, 92
Acts 16:31, 81
Acts 26:20, 82
Romans 5:19, 83
Romans 6:13, 84
Romans 8:1–6, 84
Romans 12:1–2, 6, 75
Romans 15:30–32, 86
1 Corinthians 12–14, 76
2 Corinthians 1:1–5, 92, 107
2 Corinthians 3:17–18, 84
2 Corinthians 3:18, 75
2 Corinthians 5:17, 74, 88, 89
2 Corinthians 7:9–10, 82
Ephesians 2:8–10, 81
Ephesians 3:17–18, 89
Ephesians 4:13, 96

Ephesians 4:17–24, 75
Ephesians 5:18, 84
Ephesians 6:18, 84
Colossians 3:1–17, 75
1 Thessalonians 5:17, 86
1 Timothy 2:1–10, 86
Hebrews 2:11–13, 88
Hebrews 10:24–25, 84
Hebrews 12:3–13, 84
Hebrews 13:5, 93
James 1:17, 87
1 Peter 1:5, 84
1 Peter 1:11, 78
2 Peter 1:4, 88
Second Chance Trust (SCT), 66
selective coding, 100
self-awareness, 49
self-directed learning, 36–37, 66
self-discovery, 112, 117
self-examination with others, 35, 41, 48, 102
self-reflective learning
    defined, 36–37
    outcome of, 64–65, 104–5
    processes operating within, 37
    transformation through, 72, 102, 117
self-reliance, 66
self-transformation, 66
self-understanding, 50, 69
Selzer, Elizabeth, 54–56
seminary training, 54–56
semi-transitive thought, 35
Senegal, 3
Senghor, Léopold Sédar, 40
sense of community, 52
service learning, 39
Sethi, Meera, 28
Sheldrake, Philip, 57–58
Sierra Leone, 14–15
Sifuna, Daniel Namusonge, 10
Singapore study of bereaved youth, 60–61
Smallbones, Jackie L., 94, 106
Small Groups experience of TM Program, 54, 55
social commitment, 52
social/community transformation

Index

church as venue for, 8, 110, 112–13, 114
educational system fostering, 63–67, 69, 110
example of, 3
as fruit of salvation, 83–84
as goal of education, 10
through education, 8
work of study graduates, 105
See also community transformation
societal context. *See* context
socio-cultural challenges, 18–21, 31
sociolinguistic distorted assumptions, 64, 65
sociolinguistic meaning perspective, 38
socio-political empowerment, 63
Solomon, Nicky, 67
South Africa, 23, 28–29, 65
South African Qualifications Authority, 29
spiritual dimension of transformative learning, 38, 56–63
spiritual formation, 81
spirituality
of Africans, 14
in African worldview, 114
as coping mechanism, 60–61
defined, 57–58
effect on processing and interpretation of events, 39–40
spirituality-focused coping, 60
spiritual transformation
of graduate students, 109
outcome of, 105
through life-crisis triggers, 58–63
triggers for, 84–92, 104–5, 117
See also Biblical view of holistic transformation
Spivak, Gayatri Chakravorty, 105
Starcher, Richard L., 8
STEM courses, linked, 45–46
Steyn, H. J., 23
Stokes, C. Shannon, 20–21
straightforward reflection, 40
Strauss, Anslem L., 78
Striano, Maura, 5
Student Engagement and Perception of Campus Environment, 52–54
students
academic success in learning communities, 52–56
integration of faith and learning and, 62
relationships of transformative students, 35
relationships with teachers, 45–47, 49–51
reliance on teachers, 34–35
school attendance, 3–4, 20–21, 24, 31–32
study of holistic transformation in Kenya
advantages of, 7–9
comparison of findings with Biblical teaching on transformation, 105–7
comparison of graduates from Christian and public universities, 107
context and method, 97–100
description of sampled universities, 119–21
hypothesis summarizing findings, 110–13
implication for theory, research, and practice, 113–14
integration of findings with theory and literature on transformative learning, 100–101t, 100–105, 117
integration of finding with research questions, 107–10
letter to and responses from sampled universities, 124–29
limitations of, 116
pilot study at Biola University, 98
profile of interview participants, 130–31t
rationale for, 4–9
recommendations for educational practice in Africa, 114–16, 118
recommendations for further research, 116–17, 118
research questions, 97–98, 122–23
summary, 117–18
theme of, 100, 109, 110, 117
subjective reframing, 42, 43
subjective theory, 98

Index

Sub-Saharan Africa, 8–9, 20–21. *See also specific country*
suffering, 92–93
support network, 59–60
synthesis, 43
systematic critical self-reflection on assumptions, 42
Szirmai, Adam, 7

tais proseuchais (public prayer), 86
Talmud, 89
Tanzania, 30–31
taxonomy of cognitive domain, 42–43
taxonomy of critical reflection, 42–43
Taylor, Edward W., 77
Taylor, W. H., 14, 48, 113, 117
teachers
  as agent of transformation, 96
  attrition of, 26–27, 28
  authenticity of, 49
  critical thinking skills of, 29–31
  economic challenges affecting shortages, 26–27, 28, 32
  education of, 28
  integration of faith and learning, 62
  migration of, 25, 28–29, 32
  overloaded classes for, 26, 27, 30
  practices for facilitating engagement with black students, 46–47
  relationships with students, 13, 35, 45–46, 49–51
  role in integration of spirituality into education, 62
  self-understanding of, 49
  student reliance on, 34–35
  training for, 28
  See also academics
technical learning, 36
Tedeschi, Richard, 58, 59, 60
Teferra, Damtew, 28
themes
  coding of, 106
  defined, 99
  of Kenya study, 100, 109, 110, 117
theological education (Nigeria), 22–23. *See also* Peter, Saint
theoretical knowledge, 80
theory, implications for, 113–14
theory of education for holistic transformation, 33–70
  affective/relational dimension of transformative learning, 48–56
  critical reflection in, 40–47
  experiential learning, 67–68
  integration of finding of Kenya study with, 100–101t, 100–105, 117
  origin and development of transformative learning, 34–40
  social/community transformation, 63–67
  spiritual dimension of, 56–63
therapeutic critical self-reflection on assumptions, 42
Timms, David, 87
Tisdell, Elizabeth J., 56–57
Tolliver, Derise E., 56–57
tongues, 76
Tostan (Senegal), 3
traditional education in Africa
  curriculum of, 11
  effectiveness of, 1, 3, 10–11
  example of, 2–4
  holistic aspects of, 16–17
  Kikuyu system, 18
  methodology of, 11–12, 13, 18, 103
  philosophical principles of, 12
  purpose of, 11, 18
  strengths of, 13
  study findings compared to, 104–5, 104t
  symbiosis between Western formal education and, 102, 117
  weaknesses of, 1, 12–13
transformation
  affective/relational dimension of, 48–56, 105, 106, 117
  behavioral transformation, 106
  cognitive dimension of, 34–47
  conflict transformation, 43–45
  defined, 71–75
  goal of, 57, 68, 69, 70, 102
  as God's business, 94, 106, 117
  Holy Spirit as agent of, 81, 96, 106, 109, 111, 117
  intellectual transformation, 105, 107–9

meaning transformation, 37
of points of view, 43
process of, 75–82
psycho-spiritual transformation, 58–59
role of emotions in, 79–82, 96, 105, 106
role of relationships in, 35, 45–56, 68–69, 70, 95, 102, 105, 117
as sanctification, 84–92
self-transformation, 66
social/community transformation, 63–67
spiritual dimension of, 58–63
through Christian fellowship, 87–92
through education, 7–8
through pedagogy of Peter, 75, 76–82
through prayer, 86–87
through self-discovery, 112, 117
through suffering, 92–93
through "the other" (familiar and unfamiliar), 111–12, 114, 117
through truth, 55, 71–75, 77–79, 84–86, 94, 96
through Word of God, 6, 73–75, 84–86, 111
through written material, 111, 117
triggers for, 58–62, 90–91, 95, 106
See also affective/relational dimension of transformative learning; community transformation; holistic transformation; perspective transformation; spiritual transformation; study of holistic transformation in Kenya; theory of education for holistic transformation; transformative learning
transformative learning
affective/relational dimension of, 48–56
avenues of thought, 71–75
characteristics of, 7–9, 69
collaborative learning facilitating, 52–56
in community atmosphere, 52
critical reflection in, 40–47
culture's impact on, 39
curriculum for, 4, 56–57

defined, 38–39
dimensions of, 7
goals of, 8, 65–66, 68, 69, 70
lacking in East Africa, 5
origin and development of, 34–40
pedagogical methods for, 39, 43–46, 64–65, 103
power in untransformed lives, 93
presuppositions about, 43–44
role of emotions in, 44–45
role of mentoring in, 55–56
role of relationships in, 45–47, 49–56, 68–69, 70, 102, 117
spiritual dimension of, 38, 56–63
stages of, 35, 48, 102
study of North American universities, 38–39
supporting practices and strategies for, 39
themes of successfully facilitated engagement with black students, 46–47
transformative pedagogy, 76–82
transformed faith consciousness, 58–62
transforming habits of mind, 43
transforming points of view, 43
transitional/challenges stage of learning, 44
transitional/disruptions stage of learning, 44
Trinity College, Achemota (Ghana), 17
Trueax, June, 56
trust, 45–46, 50–52, 55–56, 90–91, 96
truth
awakening of emotions, 79–82
transformation through, 55, 71–72, 73, 74–75, 77–79, 84–86, 94, 96
Word of God as, 84–86

Ubantu (humanness), 19
UBE (Universal Basic Education), 25–26
ubuntu (empathetic person), 91
Uganda, 17, 30–31
ukuntu (quality, relations), 91
umuntu (person), 91
Unger, Merrill F., 81–82
United Kingdom, migration to, 29

157

Index

United States, emigration to, 28
Universal Basic Education (UBE), 25–26
Universal Primary Education (UPE), 27
universities
  curriculum for teachers, 28
  description of those sampled, 119–21
  economic challenges, 25–28
  effectiveness of graduates, 4–5
  letter to and responses from, 124–29
  migration of academics from, 28
  reasons for choice of, 107–8, 110
  recommendations for, 115
  requirements for contribution to society, 1–2, 4
  staffing of, 25
  See also study of holistic transformation in Kenya
University of Botswana, 28
University of Nairobi (UON)
  description of, 119–20
  permission to do research, 129
  See also study of holistic transformation in Kenya
UPE (Universal Primary Education), 27
urbanization, 24, 31
Usher, Robin, 67

Van der Merwe, Marietjie, 38, 64, 65, 69
Van de Walle, Nicolas, 6–7
Verderber, Rudolph F., 90
Village Tourism and Homestead project (Abagusii village), 105
vocational training, 24

Wamukuru, D. K., 27
Ward, Kevin, 17
warm demanders, 47
Webber, Sheila Simsarian, 50
West Africa, 7, 14–16. *See also specific country*
Western formal education, 102, 117
wholisticism, 12
Wighting, Mervyn, 52
will, change of, 82
Williams, Carol J., 67
Winborne, Duvon G., 45–46
Wolhuter, C. C., 23
women
  education of, 3–4, 20–21
  Mezirow's study of community college students, 34
  role in political system, 19, 20
  role in society, 3, 24
  study of women in low-income housing in South Africa, 65
Women's Assembly, 20
Woods, Peter, 99
Word of God. *See* Bible
World Bank, 6–7
Wright, Christopher, 83
written material, 18, 110, 111, 117

Yount, William R., 42–43, 48, 67

Zajonc, A., 38
Zambia, 6, 28
Zeleza, Paul Tiyambe, 4
Zhao, Chun-Mei, 52–53
Zimbabwe, 7, 23–24, 28

www.ingramcontent.com/pod-product-compliance
Lightning Source LLC
Chambersburg PA
CBHW051938160426
43198CB00013B/2208